23 MINUTES IN HELL

23 MINUTES IN HELL

BILL WIESE

CHARISMA
HOUSE

Most Charisma House Book Group products are available at special quantity discounts for bulk purchase for sales promotions, premiums, fund-raising, and educational needs. For details, write Charisma House Book Group, 600 Rinehart Road, Lake Mary, Florida 32746, or telephone (407) 333-0600.

23 Minutes in Hell by Bill Wiese
Published by Charisma House
Charisma Media/Charisma House Book Group
600 Rinehart Road
Lake Mary, Florida 32746
www.charismahouse.com

Unless otherwise noted, all Scripture quotations are taken from the New King James Version®. Copyright © 1982 by Thomas Nelson. Used by permission. All rights reserved.

Scripture quotations marked kjv are from the King James Version of the Bible.

Scripture quotations marked tlb are from The Living Bible. Copyright © 1971. Used by permission of Tyndale House Publishers, Inc., Wheaton, IL 60189. All rights reserved.

Cover design by Justin Evans

Visit the author's website at www.soulchoiceministries.org.

International Standard Book Number: 978-1-62999-079-8.
E-book ISBN: 978-1-62999-448-2

The Library of Congress has catalogued the previous edition as follows:

Wiese, Bill.

  23 minutes in hell / Bill Wiese.-- 1st ed.

     p. cm.

  Includes bibliographical references and index.

ISBN 1-59185-882-8

1. Hell--Christianity. 2. Private revelations. I. Title: Twenty-three minutes in hell. II. Title.

BT838.W45 2006

236'.25--dc22   2005031788

ISBN-13: 978-1-59185-882-9

E-book ISBN: 978-1-59979-297-2

While the author has made every effort to provide accurate Internet addresses at the time of publication, neither the publisher nor the author assumes any responsibility for errors or for changes that occur after publication.

23 24 25 26 27 — 9 8 7 6 5

Printed in the United States of America

CONTENTS

ACKNOWLEDGMENTS

MY DEEPEST APPRECIATION to...

The Lord Jesus Christ, who has saved me from the pit of hell, for which I am eternally grateful, and has greatly blessed my life. Thank You for giving me the privilege of sharing Your Word and this testimony. My wife and I are more than honored to be part of Your great work.

Holly McClure, for your inexhaustible enthusiasm and unending support from the day Annette and I met you. It still amazes me how much God blessed that initial interview on your radio talk show in 1999. Your dedication, expertise, friendship, and commitment to us are most appreciated and highly valued. God's way of granting you "unusual access" to share this message continues to amaze us!

Mike Paquette, for your unwavering commitment to this work and for helping me with so many aspects of this ministry. You are a most trusted friend who takes the words *loyalty* and *dedication* to a new level. Your "nothing is impossible" attitude is always admired. I thank the Lord so very much for my having met you.

Hal Linhardt, for your commitment to the Lord and for sharing this testimony with countless others, which has resulted in many salvations. Thank you for your endless support and friendship.

Dane Bundy, for your excellent research on many of the scriptures and your humble attitude. Thank you, Dane!

My very good friend Greg, who is more like a brother. I value your friendship, support, and integrity more than you'll ever know. Your character and ethics are exemplary. Over the years the insight I have gained during our many "character" discussions has greatly impacted my life and has served as a reminder in some of life's most difficult tests.

My father-in-law, Stan, whose assistance with the real estate business and computers I could not do without. Your excellent work ethic, dedication, and positive attitude have helped us both through many challenges and deadlines! I am proud to have such a godly man as part of my family.

The many others who have prayed for us: our families and our dear friends, especially Steve and Kelly, Lou, and Pastors Raul and Sharon. Your friendship is valued beyond words. You truly are covenant friends.

Lastly, my beautiful and exceptional wife, Annette, without whom the book would not have been possible. Your many hours of prayer, unwavering faith, commitment, and support have been invaluable. I have been blessed with truly the greatest wife a man could ever dream of. I will love you forever, my lady of honor.

It is my desire that this book will cause you to examine the single most important issue you will ever face and that it will help you make the right decision.

—BILL

FOREWORD

THERE HAVE BEEN numerous times throughout my life when God has divinely appointed people who have forever changed and edified me. Meeting Bill and Annette Wiese was one of those "God moments" for me.

I met Bill and his beautiful wife, Annette, when I was a movie critic for several media outlets and had an evening radio talk show, *Holly McClure Live*, in San Diego, California. One day a mutual friend called and recommended that I interview a man who had come to her Bible study and told of an amazing experience God had given him in hell. At the time, I produced my own show, and since Halloween was fast approaching, I thought the subject of someone claiming he went to hell and saw demons would at the very least make for a great radio show.

After agreeing to have Bill on without ever having met him, I naturally had some concerns about his story and wasn't sure how he would come across to my listening audience. But after calling him and listening to a brief description of what he went through, I knew within minutes that he was telling the truth. His humble manner and godly character were immediately transparent as his soothing voice calmly relayed his harrowing experience. When I hung up, I knew that instead of simply making a great radio show, Bill's message would end up being so much more. God had a powerful plan and unseen purpose not only for that hour but also for the friendship that lay ahead.

I opened my show with a sobering reminder that my guest and his subject were not a joke or a hoax. I mentioned how our culture has trivialized the subject of hell to such an extent that we, in fact, celebrate with devil costumes, demonic masks, and candy on Halloween, the second most commercialized holiday in America. I added that Bill's experience was a different side of hell, one they'd never heard before, one that was terrifying, real, and permanent. I told them that Bill's testimony would more than likely change their lives forever. Then we began the show.

For the entire hour Bill told about his journey to hell, I was enthralled and mesmerized with his detailed account. I took no phone calls. At the end of the show we simply gave out his pager number because he didn't have a ministry, website, book, or phone number for people to call. By the time I closed my show Bill's pager was buzzing nonstop. "Journey to Hell" was one of my most popular shows. I received numerous requests for tapes and a barrage of phone calls and e-mails asking me to replay Bill's story in the weeks and months that followed. Bill received testimony after testimony of how his message had changed people's lives. Some of those stories are featured in this book.

As we sat in my studio that night, we knew something wonderful had just happened. Each of us felt the presence of God hovering over that show, and we knew that God was working to change the hearts, minds, and lives of those who had tuned in for even a few brief moments. We likewise knew God had divinely brought us together for a greater purpose than simply an "appearance" on a radio show. That night I pledged my willingness to do everything in my power to help Bill get his story told.

I've been a film critic since the late 1980s, so I've reviewed thousands of movies. I can assure you that just as there are countless people of faith who ask God to help them write or create a spiritual message in films, it's not hard to imagine that there are likewise countless screenwriters and special effects artists who may have been influenced by the demonic realm to realistically portray demons and the hellish underworld. Our culture has become desensitized and conditioned to accept various forms of demonic creatures, caricatures of Satan, and glimpses of hell as simply "entertainment."

Remember when the word *hell* used to be considered a curse word? My younger sister repeated what she learned from the neighborhood boys and got her tongue swabbed with a bar of soap—just for saying *hell*. Oh, how times have changed! These days the word has permeated our culture. *Hell* is hardly considered a curse word or even a "bad" word, and it has steadily become part of our cultural slang, a figure of speech that has crept into our everyday vocabulary. Television and movies have inundated us with the use of the word so that we hardly notice when it's being used. How many times have you heard a character say, "Go to hell," or, "Hell, no!," or someone casually use a phrase such as "hot as hell" in everyday discussions?

Since the significance of the word has been culturally watered down, it would be reassuring to find the true definition, impact, and consequences of hell preached from our nation's pulpits. But the hellfire-and-brimstone message of Dante's *Inferno* that was taught years ago in various denominations is no longer a popular subject with modern-day "religiously correct" churches. In fact, hell is considered "too negative" for most preachers, who are afraid of scaring away their growing congregations. The idea that a person could actually spend eternity in hell seems to have been deleted from the church, along with moral absolutes.

Although America is generally considered a Christian nation, in fact, there are a large number of people who are non-Christian or practice no religion at all. A recent poll asked more than a thousand Americans about the subject of eternal life, and 67 percent believed that their souls would go to heaven or hell when they died, while 24 percent did not believe that either heaven or hell even existed. That statistic—the people who don't believe heaven or hell exists—is why I'm passionate about sharing Bill's story. God has sent Bill with a wake-up message for you and those you love because God doesn't want anyone to spend eternity without Him.

Hell is a real place, but telling people they might go there is not an easy or popular message. God knew what He was doing when He gave Bill the difficult task of sharing his story. He knew that Bill's character, his integrity, his faith, and his godly wife, who supports him with her amazing prayers, would guard the message with truth and protect it with honor. I am blessed to have met Bill and Annette and to call them friends. I am privileged to be a part of this extraordinary gift from God.

—Holly McClure

PREFACE TO THE TENTH-ANNIVERSARY EDITION OF *23 MINUTES IN HELL*

IT HAS BEEN an amazing ten years since the release of *23 Minutes in Hell*. Annette and I never could have imagined that this book would reach around the world and be published in nine languages. But the book was just the beginning of a growing ministry that would eventually take us to countless domestic and international locations to speak, have us conduct hundreds of live meetings, and allow us to appear on over four hundred radio talk shows and give eighty television interviews. The most important aspect of all, however, has been the changed lives.

We have witnessed tens of thousands of people give their lives to Jesus! We have also seen countless Christians recommit to sharing their faith, enter into ministry, and spread the message of *23 Minutes in Hell*. Hundreds of people have approached us at our meetings to share how our books, ministry, or videos have impacted their lives.

Among the stories was one from a woman who shared that she read my book, received Christ, and the very next day witnessed to and led her neighbor to Christ. The following day her neighbor died in an automobile accident. Imagine that—a one-day-old Christian was motivated to share her faith immediately. Amazing! And it's a good thing she did.

Another woman shared with me that her best friend was going to commit suicide the night before. She gave her friend my book, which her friend read, and then she invited her friend to come to a church in her area the next morning. I just happened to be speaking at that very church that day. What are the chances of that? The friend came forward and gave her heart to Jesus.

There have been many others who have shared that they too decided not to commit suicide after reading this book. Only the Holy Spirit could have that kind of influence on someone. We believe it is the scripture in the book that arrests their hearts.

Something we've noticed too is the growing number of youths being impacted by this book's message. For example, at a recent meeting a five-year-old girl approached me and said, "I went forward and gave my heart to Jesus today. I want to be a missionary like you. I'm joining this church today, and I bought two of your books!" She was so bold and definite about her path.

In a recent letter one seventeen-year-old shared with me that he read my book when he was ten years old. Now he had shared it with his entire dorm of fifty students and was leading a Bible study for the hundreds of students who attend his school. Like so many others, he has developed a passion to share God's Word and, as he put it, "help others avoid the lake of fire." This is what has motivated him.

It's because of stories such as these that God continues to increase the reach of this ministry. We believe the reason for the book's success is that it helps prevent people from going to hell through the use of hundreds of scriptural references. It is God's desire that people would turn from sin, confess Jesus Christ as their Lord and Savior, and go to heaven. It is hard to believe that God could use an unknown, conservative person such as me to further His message, but He has, and He continues to do so.

Annette and I have been privileged to meet many wonderful pastors along this journey, as well as countless exceptional people. While we will continue to travel by God's direction, we also have seen tremendous growth in the use of media to reach people. God continues to open new doors of possibility for the message of *23 Minutes in Hell* to be shared.

Our prayer is that the members of the body of Christ would honor one another and work together to fulfill the Great Commission. As Christians we are all part of one team, and we need one another to share the message of salvation. The consequence of not doing so is eternal hell for those who are not reached.

We are honored to do what God has called us to do, and we are grateful for the many amazing letters and testimonies we've received. We are thankful for the interest so many people have shown in this message and for the support and the loving encouragement they have offered us. As one who did not want to be identified with anything supernatural and was admittedly uncomfortable sharing his experience, I can tell you that only God could have brought about all that has taken place.

I have always said it is not important whether people believe my experience. It is only important that they check out for themselves what the Bible has to say about hell and avoid it just the same. I am just a signpost to point people to the Scriptures.

We remain in His humble service.

—BILL WIESE

A WORD OF WARNING

ON SUNDAY, NOVEMBER 22, 1998, my wife, Annette, and I spent the evening at the home of one of our close friends. There was nothing unusual about that night. Annette and I headed home at around 11:00 p.m., and we fell into bed shortly before midnight, unaware that my life was about to be changed forever by an event I still find hard to explain. Hours later I woke up and got out of bed to get a drink of water. I glanced at the clock and saw that it was 3:00 a.m. Then, without any notice, I found myself being hurled through the air and then falling to the ground, completely out of control.

I landed in what appeared to be a prison cell. The walls of the cell were made out of rough-hewn stone and had a door made of what appeared to be thick metal bars.[1] I was completely naked, which added to the vulnerability of a captive. This was not a dream—I was actually in this strange place. Fully awake and cognizant, I had no idea what had happened, how I had traveled, or why I was there until it was shown to me and explained later during my journey.

The very first thing I noticed was the temperature. It was hot—far beyond any possibility of sustaining life. It was so hot that I wondered, *"Why am I still alive? How could I survive such intense heat?"*[2] My flesh should have disintegrated off my body. The reality was it didn't. This wasn't a nightmare; it was real. The severity of this heat had the effect of taking every ounce of strength out of me.

I wasn't yet fully aware of it—but I had fallen into hell.

If you are like most people, you probably opened this book out of pure curiosity. Somewhere in the back of your mind you may be thinking, *"Did this man really go to hell—hell as in fire, burning, and torment?"* Or maybe you think I'm making the whole thing up because no one could go to hell and live to tell about it. You might not even believe there is a hell. If you do believe in a literal hell, you probably think the only reason God would send someone to hell is if that person was evil and deserved it, right?

Well, in my case it's none of the above. Yes, I was taken to a literal burning hell, and no, it had nothing to do with being *good* or *bad*. The reason I was shown this place was to bring back a message of warning. My story is not one that seeks to condemn you but rather to inform you that hell is a real place—it does exist. God's desire is that no one go there. But the sad and simple fact is people make the choice to go to hell every day.

Today in our society warnings serve to protect us from harm. Not only are warnings welcome guideposts, but also we expect them to be posted on everything from toothpaste to real estate. For instance, in the real estate industry contracts are written to protect the buyer and disclose to that buyer all facts known. In fact, the buyer would be outraged if he or she were not given full disclosure.

What loving parent does not warn his or her children not to play in a busy street?

When the sky turns dark and the winds increase, we look to our local news channel to communicate tornado or hurricane warnings.

So why is it that when God warns us of what will happen if we travel down the wrong road, we are quick to say He is myopic and condemning? Or we say He is judgmental! The truth is He warns us because He is a good God, one who loves us and wants to help, guide, and protect us. Personally His warnings are most welcome in my life.

This experience is not something I asked for or ever wanted. Being of a conservative nature, being associated with something seemingly so radical is not comfortable for me. However, I am able to overlook my discomfort in light of God's overall perspective. I have since discovered that my story coincides with what Scripture details about hell. This is of far greater importance than what I have to say.

My horrifying journey felt like it lasted an eternity, but in actuality it lasted less than half an hour. Those twenty-three minutes were more than enough to convince me that I would never, ever want to return, not even for one more minute. And it has now become my life's purpose to tell others what I saw, heard, and felt so that whoever reads this story will be able to take the proper measures to steer clear of this place at all costs.

My sincere hope is that this book is the closest you will ever come to experiencing this reality for yourself.

INTRODUCTION NOTES

1. "They shall go down to the bars of the pit" (Job 17:16, KJV). "The earth with her bars was about me for ever: yet hast thou brought up my life from corruption" (Jon. 2:6, KJV).

2. "For a fire is kindled in My anger, and shall burn to the lowest hell" (Deut. 32:22). "...suffering the vengeance of eternal fire" (Jude 7).

[PART I]

MY EXPERIENCE IN HELL

THE CELL

O N OUR FIRST anniversary Annette and I took a trip to Carmel, California. It was a perfect place to celebrate, sitting on the outdoor deck of one of our favorite spots overlooking the picturesque mountain cliffs, trees, and homes edged along the blue Pacific. The crystal-clear morning sky and waves hitting the shoreline were a perfect backdrop for shared conversations about our hearts' desires, goals, and dreams for our new life together. I mentioned to my wife, "This is probably the closest place to heaven anyone could experience while on the earth." Annette agreed. We both had a strong feeling that God had put us together for a very special purpose.

As we reflected on the goodness of God in our lives, one word summed up the attitude of my heart: *grateful.* I was so very grateful for my beautiful wife and the life we had together. From the moment I saw her, I knew she was the one for me, and I truly view her as a gift from above. I was grateful for my health, family, bills paid, financial provision, and peace. There is something deeply satisfying when one has such moments to reflect and dream. What would be the next chapter to unfold in our lives? Just two weeks later, unbeknownst to us, we would be confronted with an event that would forever change our lives.

THE JOURNEY

I've already shared with you the beginning of that journey that happened on November 22, 1998. That was the night I was catapulted into the very pit of hell. My point of arrival was a cell that was approximately fifteen feet high by ten feet wide with a fifteen-foot depth.

With its walls of rough stone and rigid bars on the door, I felt as though I was in a temporary holding area, a place where a prisoner would await his final hours before meeting a far more terrifying destiny. Isaiah 24:22 says, "And they shall be gathered together, as prisoners are gathered in the pit, and shall be shut up in the *prison*" (KJV, emphasis added). Proverbs 7:27 refers to "chambers" of death in hell.

As I lay there on the floor of that cell, I felt extremely weak. I noticed that I had a body, one that appeared just as it is now.[1] Lifting my head, I began to look around. Immediately I realized that I was not alone in this cell. I saw two enormous beasts unlike anything I had ever seen before.

These creatures were approximately ten to thirteen feet tall.[2] These towering beasts were far, far beyond intimidating. It is one thing to be threatened by someone much taller than you. But these creatures were not of this natural world. I recognized that they were entirely evil, and they were gazing at me with pure, unrestrained hatred, which completely paralyzed me with fear. "Evil" and "Terror" stood before me. Those creatures were an intensely concentrated manifestation of those two forces.

I know of no one who has overstated the terror of Hell.... We
are meant to tremble and feel dread. We are meant to recoil
from the reality. Not by denying it, but by fleeing from it into
the arms of Jesus, who died to save us from it.[3] —JOHN PIPER

I still had no idea where I was, and I felt utterly panicked. Although I had no point of reference, no familiarity with anything I was experiencing, and no understanding of how I got there, still I was faced with the unimaginable reality that a tortuous death seemed certain.

The creatures weren't animals, but they weren't human either. Each giant beast resembled a reptile in appearance but took on human form. The beasts' arms and legs were unequal in length, out of proportion—without symmetry. The first one had bumps and scales all over its grotesque body. It had a huge protruding jaw, gigantic teeth, and large sunken-in eyes.[4] This creature was stout and powerful, with thick legs and abnormally large feet. It was pacing violently around the cell like a caged bull, and its demeanor was extremely ferocious. The second beast was taller and thinner, with very long arms and razor-sharp fins that covered its body. Protruding from its hands were claws that were nearly a foot long. Its personality seemed different from the first being. It was certainly no less evil, but it remained rather still.

I could hear the creatures speaking to one another. Although I could not identify what language it was, somehow I could understand their words. They were awful words— terrible, blasphemous language that spewed from their mouths, expressing extreme hatred for God.[5]

Suddenly they turned their attention toward me. They

3

looked like hungry predators staring at their prey. I was terrified. Like an insect in a deadly spider's web, I felt helpless, trapped, and frozen with fear. I knew I had become the object of their hostility, and I felt a violent, evil presence as I had never felt before and greater than anything I could imagine. They possessed a hatred that far surpassed any hatred a person could have, and now that hatred was directed straight at me. I couldn't identify what these beasts were yet, but I knew they meant me harm.[6]

I wanted desperately to get up and run. But as I lay on that wretched cell floor, I noticed that I had absolutely no strength in my body. I could barely move. Why didn't I have strength? I felt so defenseless.[7] Psalm 88:4 says, "I am counted with them that go down into the pit: I am as a man that hath *no strength*" (KJV, emphasis added).

I knew it was much more than physical weakness I was feeling. Indeed, it was weakness of every form. I was mentally and emotionally drained, even though I had only been there a few minutes. Most of us have experienced a loss of strength and energy after intense weeping, emotional distress, or grief. After a time of healing we regain that strength, though it may take years. However, at that moment I felt that there would never be a time for recuperating from the literal weight that had fallen upon me—a weight of hopeless despair.

For hell is viewed by our Lord Jesus Christ not as "made for man," but "made for the devil and his angels." Humans as such were made for fellowship with God and for eternal glory. That such creatures should be banished forever into the outer darkness with no escape exit, should fill us with a sense of horror.[8] —SINCLAIR B. FERGUSON

Two more creatures came into the cell, and I had the feeling these four beings had been "assigned" to me. I felt as though I was being "sized up" and that my torment would be their amusement. As they entered, suddenly the light vanished. It became absolutely pitch-black. I had no idea why the sudden and intense darkness had begun. But I sensed that the light that had been present had been an intrusion and that the atmosphere had now returned to its normal state of darkness. Lamentations 3:6 states, "He has set me in *dark places* like the dead of long ago" (emphasis added).

One of the creatures picked me up. The strength of the beast was amazing. I was comparable to the weight of a water glass in its hand. Mark 5:3–4 describes a man possessed with a demon with these words: "No one could bind him, not even with chains... the chains had been pulled apart by him, and the shackles broken in pieces." Instinctively I knew that the creature holding me had strength approximately one thousand times greater than a man. I cannot explain how I perceived that bit of information.

Then the beast threw me against the wall. I crumbled onto the floor. It felt as though every bone in my body had been broken.[9] I felt pain, but it was also as if the pain was being softened somehow. I knew I did not experience the full brunt of the pain. I thought, "How was it blocked?"

The second beast, with its razor-like claws and sharp protruding fins, then grabbed me from behind in a bear hug. As it pressed me into its chest, its sharp fins pierced my back. I felt like a rag doll in its clutches in comparison with his enormous size. He then reached around and plunged his claws into my chest and ripped them outward. My flesh hung from my body like ribbons as I fell again to the cell floor.[10] These creatures had no respect for the human body—how remarkably it is made. I have always taken care of myself by eating right, exercising, and staying in shape, but none of that mattered, as my body was being destroyed right before my eyes.

I knew I could not escape this torture via death, for not even that was an option. Death penetrated me but eluded me. The creatures seemed to derive pleasure in the pain and terror they inflicted upon me. Psalm 116:3 (KJV) says, "The sorrows of death compassed me, and the pains of hell gat hold upon me: I found trouble and sorrow." Oh, how I yearned for death, but there would be none.

THE LIVING DEAD

I pleaded for mercy, but they had none—absolutely no mercy. They seemed to be incapable of it. They were pure evil. No mercy existed in that place. Mercy is from God in heaven.[11]

The mental anguish I felt was indescribable. Asking for mercy from such evil only seemed to heighten their desire to torment me more.

I was conscious of the fact that there was no fluid coming from my wounds. No blood, no water, nothing.[12] At this time I did not stop to wonder why. I was extremely nauseated from the terrible, foul stench coming from these creatures. It was absolutely disgusting, foul, and rotten. It was by far the most putrid smell I had ever encountered.[13] If you could take every rotten thing you can imagine, such as an open sewer, rotten meat, spoiled eggs, sour milk, dead and rotting animal flesh, and sulfur, and magnify it a thousand times, you might come close. This is not an exaggeration. The odor was actually extremely toxic, and that alone should have killed me.

The reality of Hell is so far beyond our experience that language cannot adequately describe it.[14] —EDWARD DONNELLY

Instinctively I just knew that some of the things I was experiencing were a thousand times worse than what would be possible on the earth's surface—things such as the odors mentioned, the strength of the demons, the loudness of the screams, the dryness, and the loneliness I felt.

Somehow I managed to move a bit and dragged myself across the ground toward the barred door. I couldn't see, but I remembered the direction of the door that had been left open. I finally made it to the door and crawled out of the cell. For whatever reason the creatures allowed me to crawl out without stopping me.

As soon as I exited the cell, my first instinct was to get as far away as possible. Again, I desperately wanted to run. All I could think of was to get up onto my feet. However, every move to get up took great effort. I remember wondering, "Why is this so difficult?" After tremendous exertion I was finally able to stand. I was thoroughly exhausted and, at the same time, very frustrated at how hard simple movement had become. Although I was now outside the cell, I could not run, and fear continued to bind itself around me as a snake constricting its prey.

I was horrified as I heard the screams of an untold multitude of people crying out in torment. It was absolutely deafening. The terror-filled screams seemed to go right through me, penetrating my very being. I once heard about a television special where a news reporter spent the night in a prison just to experience prison life firsthand. The prisoners were crying, moaning, and yelling all night long. He stated that he couldn't sleep because of all the noise. This place where I now stood was far, far worse.

Through the panic and the deafening noise I struggled to gather my thoughts. "I'm in hell! This is a real place, and I'm actually here!" I frantically tried to understand, but it was just so inconceivable. "Not me. I'm a good person," I thought. The fear was so intense, I couldn't bear it, but again, I couldn't die.[15] I knew that most people up on the surface of the earth did not believe or even know that there was a whole world going on down here. They wouldn't believe it. But here it existed, and it was all too real. This place was so terrifying, so intense, and so hostile that it would be impossible for me to exaggerate the horror.

I did not know how I had arrived there. The fact that I *knew God* was kept from my mind. This was explained to me later by the Lord Himself. In retrospect I know there are several scriptures indicating that God does sometimes hide things from man's mind.[16]

As I stood outside the cell, I actually felt the darkness. Exodus 10:21 speaks of "darkness which may even be felt." It was not like the darkness on the earth. I was once in a coal mine in Arizona that was completely void of light. I couldn't see anything, yet it was nothing like the darkness in hell.[17] It was as though the darkness in hell had its own power, a power that consumed me.[18] The darkness was not simply the absence of light—it had a distinctive evil presence, a feeling of death, a penetrating evil.

Hell is a place of unrelieved torment and horrible misery...a place of impenetrable darkness...a place of fire...a place of unrelieved torment for both body and soul. Hell will be horrible for everybody there, but some people will suffer more than others.[19] —JOHN MACARTHUR

I looked off to my right and could faintly see flames from afar that dimly lit the skyline. I knew the flames were coming from a large pit, a gigantic raging inferno approximately one mile in diameter and about ten miles away. This was just one of the many things I simply knew. My senses were keener.[20]

The flames were intense, but the darkness seemed to swallow up the light.[21] The skyline was barely visible. The darkness was somewhat like a black hole. I have heard scientists say that within our universe's black holes the pull of gravity is so strong that it actually stops light from traveling, and it cannot escape from the hole. The darkness in hell is like that. It is so dark that it seems to hinder any light from traveling.

The only visible area was that which the flames exposed. The ground was all rock, barren and desolate. There was not one green thing, not one living thing, not one blade of grass, not one leaf on the ground—it was just a complete wasteland.[22] In Ezekiel 26:20 we read, "Then I will bring you down with those who descend into the Pit...and I will make you dwell in the lowest part of the earth, in places desolate from antiquity, with those who go down to the Pit." On earth even deserts contain life that has adapted to its harsh environment, and they have a natural beauty. But the place I saw was barren—nothing like the desert.

One of the most painful thoughts I had was the realization that I could never get to my wife. She had no idea of my existence in this place. I would never, ever see her again. I couldn't even explain or tell her of my doom. My wife and I are extremely close, and I used to tell her that if there was ever a disaster on the earth and we were apart that day, I would find a way to get to her. I would stop at nothing to get to her. Now to never see her again was so inconceivable to me.[23] I understood that I would never, ever get out. In Psalm 140:10 we read, "Let burning coals fall upon them; let them be cast into the fire, into deep pits, that *they rise not up again*" (emphasis added). I couldn't even tell her what had happened, and that knowledge alone was too much to endure.

It is an experience of intense anguish...a sense
of loneliness....There is the realization that this
separation is permanent....Thus, hopelessness comes
over the individual.[24] —MILLARD J. ERICKSON

The air was filled with smoke, and a filthy, deathly, decaying odor hung in the oxygen-depleted atmosphere.[25] It seemed as if all the oxygen had been sucked up by the high-leaping flames in the distance. I could barely breathe. The lack of oxygen in the atmosphere left me gasping for every little bit of air I could inhale. There was no humidity or moisture in the air. It was exhausting even to try to get just one breath.

One of the worst sensations I experienced was an insatiable thirst and dryness. I was so extremely thirsty. My mouth was so dry it felt as if I had been running through the desert for days. There was no water, no humidity in the air—no water anywhere. I desperately longed for just one drop of water.[26] Like with the man in torment in Luke 16:23, just one drop of water would have been so precious to me. It is difficult to conceive of a world without any water. It would truly be most miserable. It is impossible for any of us to imagine such extreme dryness. Water has always been very valuable and pleasurable to my wife and me, and now so much more so. Water is a life-giving substance, and in hell there is no life of any kind. All is dead.

With thoughts of utter hopelessness flooding my mind, I looked out at the desolate, barren cavern toward the flames. All the memories of what a wonderful life I had enjoyed were now a world apart, just things of the past. There was no work, no goals, no wisdom, and no opportunity to speak to anyone or to solve any problem. There was no need to offer advice, help, or comfort of any kind. Purpose was nonexistent. All life was over, and a useless "wasting away" permeated my being.[27] After seeing these grotesque and deformed creatures with their jagged scales, bumps, and twisted limbs; smelling their putrid, rotting odors; and seeing the thick, smoke-filled atmosphere, I longed for my life back. I thought of my beautiful wife with her warm, loving green eyes; her zeal for life; her perfectly smooth, clear skin; and her great love for me. I missed her so deeply. I thought about us standing at the cliffs on the ocean's edge, watching the waves and ice-blue water crash onto the rocky shore. I remembered the clear skies, white clouds, sunshine, and fresh air. I yearned for her so deeply.

I wanted to talk to and interact with someone. But to have an intelligent conversation—or simply any conversation—with a human being, now so valued, was unattainable. All these things flashed through my mind. However, to entertain such memories was futile and would only lead to bitter disappointment and total frustration. How could I accept the reality I was now faced with? It was a reality filled with an eternity of pain, loss, loneliness, and doom—a most miserable existence. It would be impossible.

The lost will be "punished with everlasting destruction from the presence of the Lord" (2 Thess. 1:9). No one lives without God.... He gives you every breath you take. His kindness surrounds.... He makes the sun rise on both the evil and the good and sends rain on the unjust as well as the just (Matt. 5:45). He gives you the beauty of a summer evening, the coolness of a refreshing breeze.... He delights you with the taste of fresh crusty bread or the juice of a ripe peach. Perhaps you have experienced the ecstasy of love. These are God's gifts.... All of these are blessings from God.... But in Hell, all this will be taken from you ... all the dignity that you now have as an image bearer of God will be stripped from you.... The wicked will burn with fire but they will not be consumed.[28] —EDWARD DONNELLY

My brief moment of remembrance faded away, and once again I was faced with my present gruesome situation. My mental escape had lasted only a few seconds. I realized this horror would last for an eternity, and that knowledge thrust me back into a frantic state of mind.

I didn't even possess the thought of calling on God for help because I was there as one who didn't know God. The Lord didn't even come to mind.[29]

One of those demonic creatures grabbed me and carried me back into the cell. It threw me on the floor, and another creature quickly grabbed my head and began to crush it. Then all four of the creatures were on top of me, each grabbing a leg or an arm as if I were lifeless prey.[30] I was so far beyond terrified that there are no words to describe it.

They were just about to pull apart my body when all of a sudden I was taken out of the cell and placed next to that pit of fire I had viewed from a distance earlier.

Hell is going to be eternity filled with grief
and pain, an unquenchable fire, according to
the Bible.[31] —FRANKLIN GRAHAM

CHAPTER 1 NOTES

1. "Fear Him who is able to destroy both soul and body in hell" (Matt. 10:28). "And not that thy whole *body* should be cast into hell" (Matt. 5:29, KJV, emphasis added). "Let us swallow them alive like Sheol, and *whole*, like those who go down to the Pit" (Prov. 1:12, emphasis added).

2. It is interesting to note that Deuteronomy 3:11 speaks of the remnant of giants: "Indeed his bedstead was an iron bedstead.... Nine cubits is its length [approximately thirteen feet]." Genesis 6:4 talks about giants on the earth: "There were giants on the earth in those days, and also afterward, when the sons of God came in to the daughters of men and they bore children to them. Those were the mighty men who were of old." The term "sons of God" refers to fallen angels. Giants came as a result of evil angels in contact with women. See chapter 10, "Dealing With the Demons of Hell."

3. John Piper, "Behold the Kindness and the Severity of God," a sermon delivered June 14, 1992, at Bethlehem Baptist Church, accessed August 4, 2005, http://www.soundofgrace.com/piper92/06-14-92.htm.

4. "His soul draws near the Pit, and his life to the *executioners*" (Job 33:22, emphasis added). "I will also send against them the *teeth of beasts*, with the poison of serpents of the dust" (Deut. 32:24, emphasis added). This scripture speaks of what happened to the Israelites for their rebellion. If this is what happened to them on the

earth, how much worse will it be in hell, where His wrath is poured out?

5. "They did not like to retain God in their knowledge... being filled with all unrighteousness... murder... *haters of God... unmerciful*" (Rom. 1:28–31, emphasis added). Although these verses are referring to people, the power that influences them is demonic. Ezekiel 28:14–16 describes Lucifer with these words: "You were the anointed cherub who covers....Therefore I cast you as a *profane* thing" (emphasis added). "I am profaned [degraded, vulgar language, blasphemous] among them" (Ezek. 22:26). "Your enemies take Your name in vain" (Ps. 139:20). These are scriptures referring to people who profane the Lord, but to profane is an influence that is demonic in nature, as Ezekiel 28:14–16 states. Also, in Lester Sumrall's book *Alien Entities* he mentions the famous case of the demon-possessed girl, Clarita Villanueva, whom he confronted, stating, "There was a raging battle with the girl *blaspheming* God the Father, God the Son, and God the Holy Spirit. Her eyes were burning coals of fire and full of *hate*" (Lester Sumrall, *Alien Entities* [Springdale, PA: Whitaker House, 1995], 137, emphasis added).

6. "Nor complain, as some of them also complained, and were destroyed by the destroyer" (1 Cor. 10:10). "Delivered him to the torturers" (Matt. 18:34).

7. "Hell from beneath is excited about you, to meet you at your coming.... They all shall speak and say to you:

'Have you also become as *weak* as we?'" (Isa. 14:9–10, emphasis added).

8. Christopher W. Morgan and Robert A. Peterson, eds., *Hell Under Fire* (Grand Rapids: Zondervan, 2004), 220.

9. "Now consider this, you who forget God, lest I tear you in pieces, and there be none to deliver" (Ps. 50:22). Psalm 32:10 emphasizes the sorrows experienced: "Many sorrows shall be to the wicked." "Is it not destruction for the wicked, and disaster for the workers of iniquity?" (Job 31:3). "The adversaries of the LORD shall be broken in pieces" (1 Sam. 2:10).

10. "You who hate good and love evil; who strip the skin from My people, and the flesh from their bones" (Mic. 3:2). This verse speaks of the country's leaders doing this to the children of Israel; it is not speaking of this happening in hell. However, where do evil men get their inspiration? To support the thought of devils inflicting pain, see Mark 5:5, which mentions "cutting himself with stones." Also, 1 Kings 18:28 says, "And cut themselves...until the blood gushed out on them." In Mark 9:18–22, we read that the spirit "seizes him, it throws him down; he foams at the mouth, gnashes his teeth, and becomes rigid....And often he has thrown him both into the fire and into the water to destroy him."

11. "Your mercy, O LORD, is in the heavens" (Ps. 36:5). "The mercy of the LORD is...on those who fear Him" (Ps. 103:17).

12. "I will set your prisoners free from the waterless pit" (Zech. 9:11). "For the life of the flesh is in the blood" (Lev. 17:11). (And there is no life in hell.) "Send Lazarus that he may dip the tip of his finger in water and cool my tongue; for I am tormented in this flame" (Luke 16:24).

13. "Jesus...rebuked the foul spirit" (Mark 9:25, kjv).

14. 14. Edward Donnelly, *Heaven and Hell* (Carlisle, PA: Banner of Truth, 2002), 33.

15. "These shall be punished with everlasting destruction" (2 Thess. 1:9). "The fear of the wicked will come upon him" (Prov. 10:24).

16. Of course God can do anything, but to give scriptural references, in Luke 18:34, when Jesus was telling His disciples about being crucified and dying, we read, "This saying was hidden from them," even though Jesus had told them. After King Nebuchadnezzar lost his sanity because of sin and lived like an animal in the fields for a time, we read in Daniel 4:34, "My understanding returned to me."

17. "You have laid me in the lowest pit, in darkness, in the depths" (Ps. 88:6). "He shall go to the generation of his fathers; they shall never see light" (Ps. 49:19).

18. "When I was with you daily in the temple, you did not try to seize Me. But this is your hour, and the power of darkness" (Luke 22:53). "These are wells without water, clouds carried by a tempest, for whom is reserved the blackness of darkness forever" (2 Pet. 2:17). "His lamp

will be put out in deep darkness" (Prov. 20:20). "For whom is reserved the blackness of darkness forever" (Jude 13).

19. John MacArthur, "Hell—the Furnace of Fire," Tape #GC2304.

20. In *One Minute After You Die,* Erwin W. Lutzer says that those in Sheol (hell) have "heightened perception and a better understanding" (Erwin Lutzer, *One Minute After You Die* [Chicago: Moody Publishers, 1997], 39). Luke 16:23 also infers this when it speaks of the rich man in hell who "saw Abraham afar off, and Lazarus in his bosom." Being a great distance away, how could he recognize Lazarus? Or how did he recognize Abraham, whom he may not have ever known?

21. "A land as dark as darkness itself, as the shadow of death, without any order, where even the light is like darkness" (Job 10:22).

22. "We are as dead men in desolate places" (Isa. 59:10).

23. "He who goes down to the grave does not come up. He shall never return to his house" (Job 7:9–10). "The eye that saw him will see him no more" (Job 20:9).

24. *Christian Theology,* 2nd ed. (Grand Rapids: Baker Academic, 1985, 1998), 1242–43.

25. "The enemies of the LORD shall be as the fat of lambs: they shall consume; into smoke shall they consume away" (Ps. 37:20, KJV). "The smoke of their torment ascends forever and ever" (Rev. 14:11). "The sun and

the air were darkened because of the smoke of the pit"
(Rev. 9:2).

26. "Out of the pit wherein is no water" (Zech. 9:11, KJV).

27. "For there is no work or device or knowledge or wisdom
in the grave" (Eccles. 9:10). "Let them be silent in the
grave" (Ps. 31:17). "But the wicked shall be silent in
darkness" (1 Sam. 2:9). "Shall the dead arise and praise
You?...Shall Your wonders be known in the dark?...in
the land of forgetfulness?" (Ps. 88:10, 12). (What a
description of the grave, and hell is even worse!) "The
dead do not praise the LORD, nor any who go down
into silence" (Ps. 115:17).

28. Donnelly, *Heaven and Hell*, 35–37.

29. "For in death there is no remembrance of You [God];
in the grave who will give You thanks?" (Ps. 6:5). "The
dead do not praise the LORD, nor any who go down
into silence" (Ps. 115:17).

30. "Consider this, you who forget God, lest I tear you
in pieces" (Ps. 50:22). "And will cut him in two and
appoint him his portion with the unbelievers" (Luke
12:46). "And will cut him in two" (Matt. 24:51).

31. Franklin Graham, *The Name* (Nashville: Nelson Books,
2002), 20.

CHAPTER 2

THE PIT

MOMENTARY RELIEF HIT my soul as I realized I had been snatched from the grip of those hideous creatures. However, now I found myself next to an enormous pit with raging flames of fire leaping high into an open cavern. As I looked up into that dark, eerie, tomb-like atmosphere, it seemed to be like a mouth that had swallowed her dead. The flames of her ravenous appetite were never satisfied with the pitiful screams of untold multitudes.

The heat was far beyond unbearable, and I desperately wanted to escape before I too would be thrown into that inferno. As I look back on the experience now, I am reminded of the devastation of the twin towers of the World Trade Center on September 11, 2001, when some people, rather than facing the two-thousand-degree heat, chose to plummet to their death by leaping out a window. That fall, especially from such great heights, must have been horrendous. It was reported that a person subjected to that temperature would be completely incinerated in about fifteen seconds. Those people chose to make that leap rather than face the intensity of those flames for even fifteen seconds. Some scientists have reported that the core temperature at the center of the earth is approximately twelve thousand degrees. To endure that for an eternity is unfathomable.

I could see the outlines of people through the flames. The screams from the condemned souls were deafening and relentless. There was no safe place, no safe moment, no temporary relief of any kind.[1] In the media we have heard of the merciless acts of terrorists. In some cases their victims knew death would come by brutal decapitation. Try to imagine the terror these victims must have felt as they awaited their fate. In hell this state of fear never ceases for even one second. It lasts for an eternity.

There is no reason the torments of Hell could not include physical fire.[2] —ERWIN LUTZER

There were people in hell who were contained in a massive pit. Horrible creatures surrounded the perimeter. There was no way of escape. Any attempt to do so was futile. Human strength was no match for the demons. I felt such anguish for these hopeless people, but at the same time I realized I could be next.

I remember stepping into several fights as a child to protect kids who were weaker and being bullied. I was beaten up several times, but I couldn't just stand there and not help. The television actors who enforced justice and guarded the weak were my role models. Looking out for others is a godly characteristic. Since we all come from God, it is in most people to feel this way. We have seen how our country always comes to the rescue of the rest of the world. This inborn desire to protect the defenseless continued in my adult life. Now, without the ability to help even one defenseless, tormented soul, I felt the hopelessness deepen. Witnessing people in terror, in desperation, and in unending torment was more than I could bear.[3]

Now try to picture the most fearful moment of your life. For me, I remember one morning when as a teenager I was surfing off the Coast of Florida. A school of sharks showed up and surrounded us. We frantically began paddling toward the beach, and in the frenzy a guy nearby had his leg torn off. Then one shark knocked me completely off my board. My friend Rene and I were now literally swimming with the sharks. We desperately tried to get to the shore, but I sincerely felt that the blood in the water combined with the number of sharks was a certain death sentence. Suddenly a nine-foot shark grabbed my leg in its mouth and pulled me down. For seemingly no reason the shark let me go without a mark (thank God!), and Rene and I swam to shore. At the time I was an avid surfer. Needless to say, I didn't go near the water for almost two years.

Indeed, all other senses will be affected too: the ear with hideous noises, shrieks and yells from fellow damned sinners; the eye with fearful, ghastly, and horrible spectacles; the smell with suffocating odors and nasty stench, worse than that of carrion or that which comes out of an open sepulcher.[4] —THOMAS VINCENT

That was one of the most terrifying moments of my life, and that experience paled in comparison to the fear one endures for an eternity in hell. There is no way of escape. No one can rescue you.

When I had first arrived in the cell, I had noticed that I was naked, which is another form of shame and increased vulnerability. In such a hostile environment that vulnerability adds another layer of helplessness and fear to an already terrified mind.[5] In life well-adjusted, healthy people would feel shame if stripped and exposed publicly. How much more so would such shame and fear be felt in a terror-filled environment? I am reminded of the millions of Jews who were stripped naked and humiliated before being murdered with poisonous gas or cast into ovens during World War II. They experienced many tortures and humiliations, but being naked was an attempt to strip them of their dignity and to intensify their fear. Many have died horrific deaths on the earth; how much more will the torment be when it lasts forever?

The duration of Hell is endless. Although there are degrees of punishment, Hell is terrible for all the damned. The occupants are the devil, evil angels, and unsaved human beings.[6] —ROBERT PETERSON

I also experienced the misery of total exhaustion in hell. The continual emotional, mental, and physical trauma feeds this vicious cycle of sleep deprivation. You desperately long for even a few minutes of rest, but you never, ever get that privilege. Imagine for a moment how terrible you feel after only forty-eight hours of no sleep. In hell you never sleep, rest, or find a quiet moment. Any form of rest is nonexistent.[7] Even though I was only there for twenty-three minutes, the torment and trauma were so intense that I felt as if I hadn't slept in weeks. It could only worsen with time.

There is never any peace of mind.[8] There is no rest from the torments, the screams, the fear, the thirst, the lack of breath, the lack of sleep, the stench, the heat, the hopelessness, and the isolation from people.

I desperately wanted to talk to a human being, but I knew I would never get that chance.[9] You are kept from any kind of fellowship, conversation, or human interaction.

Relationships are so valuable, and it's easy to take them for granted. At the moment of death a person does not want to be surrounded by "things." That person wants to be surrounded by people who truly care for him and love him. It is extremely difficult to process the thought of knowing you will never be able to relate with anyone ever again, especially those you love. The innate, human desire to communicate, ask questions, and relate with someone who shares in your suffering is never fulfilled in hell. Instead, you are exposed only to hideous creatures. No matter who you were in life— whether famous or of great influence or a nobody—it doesn't matter. You are truly alone amidst a sea of tormented souls.

Now it is true that there are areas in this vast, fiery pit where people are thrown together, but they are only *together* in the sense that they are all experiencing the same torment. Each person is isolated in extreme agony and is screaming in fear as fire and brimstone rain down upon him. They are *together* in the same way cattle are herded into a slaughterhouse. A soul in such extreme agony would have no opportunity for a conversation. Besides, I believe everyone there is just on the verge of insanity. However, I believe you never quite go insane, for that would provide a form of escape.

And there is no escape, even mentally.

I possessed knowledge that there were different levels of torment or varying degrees of punishment.[10] I knew some people were in worse positions than others. All areas were horrid, with no place of relief or comfort. I was also aware that there were many levels far, far worse. Any level, area, or degree of torment was much worse than any concept a mind could conceive.

CHAPTER 2 NOTES

1. "But whoever listens to me will dwell safely, and will be secure, without fear of evil" (Prov. 1:33).

2. Lutzer, *One Minute After You Die*, 112.

3. "Upon the wicked He will rain coals; fire and brimstone and a burning wind shall be the portion of their cup" (Ps. 11:6–7). "And were destroyed by the destroyer" (1 Cor. 10:10). "Let burning coals fall upon them; let them be cast into the fire, into deep pits, that they rise not up again" (Ps. 140:10).

4. Thomas Vincent, *Fire and Brimstone* (Morgan, PA: Soli Deo Gloria Publications, 1999), 111–12.

5. "Sheol [hell] is naked before Him, and Destruction has no covering" (Job 26:6). This verse indicates that God can look upon hell; it's not hidden from Him. However, hell's inhabitants are also physically naked. "Blessed is he who watches, and keeps his garments, lest he walk naked and they see his shame" (Rev. 16:15). Again, the primary meaning in this verse is that without being ready and covered with the garment of salvation, we would be in shame when the Lord returns. "I counsel you to buy from Me...white garments, that you may be clothed, that the shame of your nakedness may not be revealed" (Rev. 3:18).

6. Robert Peterson, *Hell on Trial* (Phillipsburg, NJ: P&R Publishing, 1995), 201.

7. "And the smoke of their torment ascends forever and ever; and they have no rest day or night" (Rev. 14:11).

That scripture means there will be no relief from the torments and no rest—no sleep.

8. "'There is no peace,' says my God, 'for the wicked'" (Isa. 57:21). "Destruction comes; they will seek peace, but there shall be none" (Ezek. 7:25).

9. C. S. Lewis believed there would not be communication in hell because it was a place of solitude. See Lutzer, *One Minute After You Die*, 113.

10. "It will be more tolerable for the land of Sodom and Gomorrah [inferring a less tolerable situation in hell]" (Matt. 10:15). "Woe to you, scribes, and Pharisees...you will receive greater condemnation" (Matt. 23:14). "You make him twice as much a son of hell as yourselves" (Matt. 23:15). "Anyone who has rejected Moses's law dies without mercy on the testimony of two or three witnesses. Of how much worse punishment, do you suppose, will he be thought worthy who has trampled the Son of God underfoot...?" (Heb. 10:28–29). "From the lowest pit" (Lam. 3:55). "Thou hast delivered my soul from the lowest hell" (Ps. 86:13, kjv). "You have laid me in the lowest pit, in darkness, in the depths" (Ps. 88:6). See also Luke 12:42–48. See the scripture list in Appendix A. See Ezekiel 32:21–23. "These heroic personages speak from the midst of Sheol, which may suggest that they are located in the heart of the Netherworld, perhaps a more honorable assignment than 'the remotest recesses of the pit'" (Morgan and Peterson, eds., *Hell Under Fire*, 50).

CHAPTER 3

THE GATEWAY

As I stood near that enormous pit of fire, no immediate attackers seemed to be threatening, so this gave me a moment to take in my surroundings. It was raining fire and burning rock, similar to the way lava falls from the sky when a volcano explodes. The smoke from the flames was very thick, allowing visibility for only a short distance, but what I could see was horrifying. I saw many people reaching out of the pit of fire, desperately trying to claw their way out. But there was no escape.

I turned my head, and I noticed I was standing in the middle of a cave. The wall wrapped around me and led to the vast expanse of the pit. As I looked at the walls, I saw that they were covered with thousands of hideous creatures. These demonic creatures were all sizes and shapes. Some of them had four legs and were the size of bears. Others stood upright and were about the size of gorillas. They were all terribly grotesque and disfigured. It looked as though their flesh had been decomposing, and all their limbs were twisted and out of proportion. Some displayed immense, long arms or abnormally large feet. They seemed to me to be the living dead. There were also gigantic rats and huge spiders at least three feet wide and two or three feet high. I also saw snakes and worms, ranging from small to enormously large. I was petrified and could not believe my eyes.

My gaze followed the beasts up the sides of the wall, and I saw that there was a hole in the top of the cave. It was the entrance to an upward tunnel, approximately thirty-five feet in diameter. The fiendish creatures lined the tunnel walls as well. They were distinctly wicked. Their eyes were cauldrons of evil and death. Everything was filthy, stinking, rotten, and foul. There was one other distinguishing aspect about these creatures—they all seemed to possess a hatred for mankind. They were the epitome of evil. The creatures seemed to be chained, or attached in some fashion, to the cavern walls. I was relieved to know that they could not reach me.[1]

Suddenly I began ascending through the tunnel. I didn't know how I was able to ascend or why. At first I rose slowly, and as I went higher, I could view the vast wasteland of hell. I could now see more of the enormous pit, which looked to be as much as a mile across.[2] However, this was just a fraction of hell's space.[3] To the right of the large inferno were thousands of small pits, as far as I could see. Each pit was no more than three to five feet across and four to five feet deep—each pit holding a single lost soul.[4] Psalm 94:13 refers to these pits by saying, "Until the pit is dug for the wicked." As I ascended into the darkness, the fear of those horrific beasts was all encompassing.[5] I thought, "Who could fight off just one of these creatures?" No one could. Many were so massive and strong. For an instant I remembered a certain person my wife and I would see at our gym. We didn't know him, but we'd look upon him with amazement because he was so big, powerfully built, and strong. I thought, "Even he would be no match for the demons."

Continuing up, it seemed as if about thirty seconds had passed when suddenly a burst of light invaded the entire tunnel. The light was so brilliant—a pure, white light like I have never seen. It was so bright that I could not see the face of the one who was before me, but I instantly knew who He was. I said, "Jesus," and He said, "*I AM*," and I fell at His feet. It was as if I had died.[6] It seemed as if only a few moments had passed when I regained my awareness. I was still at His feet.

As I said, I didn't see His face. I saw only the outline of a man standing in a light that was so pure, bright, and, for the lack of a better word, *clean* (Ps. 19:9; Rev. 1:16–17). There really are no words to adequately describe what it was like to be in His presence. As Paul said in 2 Corinthians 12:4 about being in heaven, he heard "unspeakable words, which it is not lawful for a man to utter" (KJV).

Words also can't describe the range of emotions I experienced in the presence of the Lord. Just a moment before, I had been in the bowels of hell, just like someone who didn't know Jesus, and was cursed and damned to eternal torment.[7] As soon as He appeared, He restored an awareness to my mind that I am a Christian.[8] (He had removed the knowledge that I am a Christian in hell. I will explain the reason shortly.)

Peace had replaced terror, and safety took the place of danger. The feelings of worthlessness, shame, and humiliation disappeared as the value that He had placed on me was revealed. It was then that I truly understood how much God loves us. I was at once comforted, protected, and completely relieved.

I noticed the burden and pressure of time was gone. Here in life we seem to be in a hurry and always short of time, but in the spirit realm there is no sense of the weight of time. Time doesn't even come to mind. This is most likely because we are outside of time altogether. It felt as if a huge weight—the weight of time—had been lifted from me.

In His presence I felt His infinite power, eternal majesty, absolute authority, inexpressible love, and unsurpassed peace. There was a comfort beyond my ability to even comprehend. His voice was full of strength and yet so very compassionate. It was totally authoritative and also tender. This is actually a futile attempt to describe it and a gross misrepresentation of who He is and how it felt to be in His presence. My ability to express the greatness and awesomeness of God is extremely limited. No one could ever pen words adequate enough to express His majesty!

I just wanted to remain at His feet. I was so grateful to escape hell. I was so grateful that I do know Jesus, that I am a Christian. I just wanted to worship Him. Looking back, I now realize that the light that was present when I was dropped into the cell was, in fact, the Lord's presence. When He left, the cell resumed its normal state of darkness.

I remember seeing a special about the sinking of the *Titanic*. I recalled how thankful the people were to have been saved from the freezing cold water. Decades after the incident they were being interviewed, yet their appreciation for life had not diminished. Tears were flowing as each survivor recounted the story of how he or she was rescued. That's just how I felt, but much, much more so, as I knelt at the feet of Jesus. I had no words to adequately express my gratitude—I just wanted to thank Him over and over and over again.

Even though I was relieved and comforted, at the same time I felt so sinful and dirty. Standing in the presence of a holy God, I was keenly aware of my sins.

Hades is a place of torment and agony.... The judgment and Hell will be more tolerable for some than for others.... The fact that Hell will not be the same for everybody in no way implies that it will be a good place for anybody. People in Hell will be separated from God and all that is good forever. As much as I dislike the idea, I do believe that the lake of fire (Hell) is a real, literal place.[9] —CHARLES STANLEY

Jesus reached down and touched my shoulder. My strength instantly returned, and I rose to my feet. My next thought was, "Why did You send me to this awful place?"

Before I could ask the question, He answered.[10] "Because many people do not believe that hell truly exists," He told me. "Even some of My own people do not believe that hell is real." I was amazed to hear that some Christians do not believe that hell is real. I know many people think that when you die, you are annihilated, or that hell is just a state of mind. That surprises me because the Bible informs us so thoroughly on the subject. It does not teach that you are simply annihilated.[11] The teachings are very clear that hell is a place of eternal torment.[12]

I could sense the Lord's deep love for people to know the truth. Knowing that hell is a reality and how horrible it really is greatly deepens your appreciation and thankfulness. I was so, so grateful that He had rescued me.[13] But I understood that it was out of His great love for mankind that He wanted people to know this place exists, so they could instead choose life with Him. In 1 John 5:12 we are assured, "He who has the Son has life; he who does not have the Son of God does not have life."

More thoughts came to my mind. However, being in His awesome presence, I was slow to speak. But before I could get the questions out of my mouth, He would answer. Psalm 139:2, 4 says, "You understand my thought afar off....For there is not a word on my tongue, but behold, O LORD, You know it altogether." There have been times shared with my wife when I was thinking about something, and she would bring up exactly what I was thinking about at that moment. Other times we just sense what the other is about to say or do in a given situation. After something like this happens to us, one of us will tell the other, "I knew exactly what you were thinking, and I thought you'd say that." I believe that *oneness* is part of what makes marriage so special. The marriage relationship is to be a parallel of what the Lord wants with each one of us—a deep, intimate relationship where you share one another's emotions, insights, desires, and thoughts.

As I stood there before the Lord, I thought, "Why did You choose me for this experience?" There was no answer. To this day I still do not fully understand why the Lord decided to choose me. In many ways it doesn't seem to make sense. First of all, I'm a Realtor, not a Billy Graham or Mother Teresa. Second, I love order, cleanliness, and quiet, and hell is the antithesis of those things. I know most people appreciate order, cleanliness, and tranquility; however, I am more fanatic about those things than most. My mother shared with me that even as a child I kept my room neat and clean and with all my toys in perfect order. I even wore three-piece suits as a child and liked it!

In addition, my wife and I disdain horror movies and never attend them. We make every effort to keep any evil influence out of our home and away from our lives. And besides all that I don't even like the summertime. Summer is even too hot for me!

Jesus said to me, "Go and tell them about this place. It is not My desire that any should go there.[14] Hell was made for the devil and his angels."[15]

I replied to Him, "Yes, of course I'll go." God's will is for all to be saved.[16] I had the most compelling desire to do His will. In His presence the things that were usually so important to me suddenly seemed so insignificant. I felt so honored to be able to do something that would please Him. Then the thought crossed my mind, "Why would anyone believe me? They will think I had a bad dream or that I am crazy."

The Scriptures speak of the "lake of fire" (Revelation 20:14), "wailing and gnashing of teeth" (Matthew 13:42), "where 'Their worm does not die and the fire is not quenched'" (Mark 9:44). If we really believe in hell, we will plead with sinners.[17] —RAY COMFORT

The Lord said to me, "It is not your job to convict their hearts. That responsibility belongs to the Holy Spirit.[18] It is your part to go and tell them." I was relieved to know that it was not my responsibility to convince anyone. He gave me the easy part—all I have to do is open my mouth and tell the people, and He draws them to Himself.

I asked, "Why did those demons hate me so much?"

He said, "Because you are made in My image, and they hate Me."[19] You see, the demons cannot harm God directly, but they can hurt His children and His creation. It saddens God to see His creation suffer.[20] The Lord loves us and wants us to live healthy, peaceful, long lives. He wants us to warn more people about hell and to share with them just what they need to do to avoid that terrible place.

I then said, "Those demons were so powerful."

He said, "All you have to do is cast them out in My name."[21]

Suddenly there in His presence the demonic creatures I had just encountered in hell now seemed so powerless. They appeared to look like ants on the wall. I thought of Pastor Raul, a dear friend, who has a God-given gift to discern demonic influence in people's lives. He understands the authority God has given us as Christians and the power of prayer. I had thought of only three people while there, and he was the third. It was Raul and his wife, Sharon's home that we had visited just the night before this happened.

It was then revealed to me that what was most important was not the power to overcome these demons, but rather, as the scripture says, "Do not rejoice in this, that the spirits are subject to you, but rather rejoice because your names are written in heaven" (Luke 10:20). The Bible says, "For the Son of man is come to seek and to save that which was lost" (Luke 19:10, KJV). The true emphasis was placed on the souls whose names were not yet written in heaven, those who were going to hell every day. I was instantly sobered as Jesus allowed me to see a steady stream of people falling through a tunnel—one after the other, after the other, after the other—into an open cavern, into the terror that I had just escaped.

While I was watching this scene, Jesus allowed me to feel just a small amount of the sorrow He feels for His creation that is going to hell.[22] His love is so far beyond our capacity and is infinitely greater than our love. I couldn't stand feeling even a fraction of the anguish He feels. I said, "Please, stop!" I couldn't bear it.

I cannot elaborate enough on this point. It was the deepest insight into God's feelings that I had during this whole experience. There's no way to measure how much He truly loves all people. When a single soul is lost to the devil and damned to that horrible place forever, it saddens Him greatly.

I would say that while I was in His presence, He allowed me to experience two of His attributes. First, there was the experience of His awesome and infinite power. To see all the billions of stars, the expansive universe, and how much He is in control of everything was overwhelming. Just think of how many stars and galaxies there are. Psalm 147:4 says, "He telleth the number of the stars; he calleth them all by their names" (KJV). They all have names—can you imagine? That alone is inconceivable. I was in awe of His majesty and power.

I looked at our planet and its vast oceans and how they do not even move (Prov. 8:29). Everything on the earth is in perfect balance and harmony. I thought about all the people who exist and how He knows how many hairs each of us has on our head (Matt. 10:30). He knows every thought and intent of our hearts (Heb. 4:12). Not a sparrow falls to the ground that He doesn't know about (Matt. 10:29). I could go on for hours about this. My point is that we serve a *big*

God, and He is not only in total control of everything but also able to answer our prayers.

The second thing He allowed me to experience was what I just mentioned: a portion of the amount of love He has for each one of us. We have all heard about His love before, but I can tell you that I never knew just how very much He loves us all. I have mentioned how much I love my wife, and it is more than I could ever express or tell you. If I told you a dozen reasons I love my wife, you would be convinced that I do, indeed, love her. If I went on for another five or six hours about how much I love her, you'd think I was a bit fanatic.

If every thought I had toward my wife represented a grain of sand, how many grains of sand would I exhaust—maybe a handful? God's thoughts for us are more than all the sand granules on the entire earth! How many thoughts would that be if each granule represented a thought? Psalm 139:17–18 says, "How precious also are Your thoughts to me, O God! How great is the sum of them! If I should count them, they would be more in number than the sand." This is literal. He loves us that much! It is amazing to feel that kind of love and that much love generating from Him. It so far surpasses our ability to love that we cannot even grasp or understand it. Ephesians 3:19 says that His love "passes knowledge."

I asked Him, "Why didn't I know You when I was there?"

He said, "I kept it from you." In order for me to experience the hopelessness of those souls in hell, the fact that I know Jesus had to be hidden from my mind. If I knew Him there, as I have since 1970, I would have had hope that He would rescue me. Experiencing the feeling of being lost forever was by far the worst part of hell. On earth we always have some form of hope. Even amidst the most dire situations we have hope that we'll escape, even if it's only through death.[23] But in hell you know positively there is no hope whatsoever; you will never get out. Your soul cannot die, and you are lost and in torment forever.[24]

Satan ... will do everything in his power to hold people captive in sin and to drag them down to the prison of eternal separation from God.[25] —BILLY GRAHAM

Finally He said, "Tell them I am coming very, very soon." In my spirit I felt an urgency to warn as many people as possible, as time is running out. He sternly said it again: "TELL THEM I AM COMING VERY, VERY SOON!" Repeating Himself tells me His coming truly is getting very, very close. Time is running out. We must get the truth out to people so they can know that there is a choice to make. Without Jesus as your Savior you will not be going to heaven, and that is absolutely certain.[26]

Looking back, I wish I would have asked Him, "What is 'very, very soon' to You, Lord?" However, when standing in the presence of almighty God, such arrogance does not come to mind. Like a soldier being commanded by his general, all I wanted to do was obey His order.

As the Lord and I were having this time together, we kept ascending the tunnel. We came to the earth's surface, and then we continued upward. We went high above the earth until we were out of the atmosphere.

CHAPTER 3 NOTES

1. One possible explanation for the demons being chained is found in Jude 6: "And the angels who did not keep their proper domain, but left their own abode, He has reserved in everlasting chains under darkness for the judgment of the great day." The creatures I encountered in hell could have been those chained fallen angels—I don't know.

2. "Then I will bring you down, with those who descend into the Pit, to the people of old, and I will make you dwell in the lowest part of the earth, in places desolate from antiquity" (Ezek. 26:20).

3. "Therefore hell hath enlarged herself" (Isa. 5:14, KJV).

4. Psalm 88:6 says, "You have laid me in the lowest pit, in darkness, in the depths." "Let burning coals fall upon them; let them be cast into the fire, into deep pits, that they rise not up again" (Ps. 140:10). "He also brought me up out of a horrible pit" (Ps. 40:2). "Let us swallow them alive like Sheol, and whole, like those who go down to the Pit" (Prov. 1:12). "Cast them down to the depths of the earth...with those who go down to the Pit" (Ezek. 32:18). "Who have gone down...to the lower parts of the earth....Now they bear their shame with those who go down to the Pit" (Ezek. 32:24).

5. "He has made me dwell in darkness, like those who have long been dead" (Ps. 143:3).

6. "His countenance was like the sun shining in its strength. And when I saw Him, I fell at His feet as dead" (Rev. 1:16–17).

7. "He will redeem his soul from going down to the Pit, and his life shall see the light" (Job 33:28). "To bring back his soul from the Pit, that he may be enlightened with the light of life" (Job 33:30).

8. "And my understanding returned to me" (Dan. 4:34).

9. Charles Stanley, *Charles Stanley's Handbook for Christian Living* (Nashville: Thomas Nelson Publishers, 1996), 245–248.

10. "You understand my thought afar off.... For there is not a word on my tongue, but behold, O LORD, You know it altogether" (Ps. 139:2, 4).

11. "And as it is appointed for men to die once, but after this the judgment" (Heb. 9:27). "These shall be punished with everlasting destruction from the presence of the Lord" (2 Thess. 1:9). "And many of those who sleep in the dust of the earth shall awake, some to everlasting life, some to shame and everlasting contempt" (Dan. 12:2). In Matthew 25:46 Jesus says, "And these will go away into everlasting punishment, but the righteous into eternal life." "And the smoke of their torment ascends forever and ever; and they have no rest day or night" (Rev. 14:11).

12. See *Hell Under Fire* and *Hell on Trial*, listed in the bibliography.

13. "Who redeems your life from destruction, who crowns you with lovingkindness and tender mercies" (Ps. 103:4).

14. "Who desires all men to be saved and to come to the knowledge of the truth" (1 Tim. 2:4). "The Lord is not

slack concerning His promise, as some count slackness, but is longsuffering toward us, not willing that any should perish but that all should come to repentance" (2 Pet. 3:9). "'As I live,' says the Lord God, 'I have no pleasure in the death of the wicked, but that the wicked turn from his way and live'" (Ezek. 33:11).

15. In Matthew 25:41 Jesus says, "Depart from Me, you cursed, into the everlasting fire prepared for the devil and his angels."

16. "He who wins souls is wise" (Prov. 11:30). "And He said to them, 'Go into all the world and preach the gospel [good news] to every creature'" (Mark 16:15). "But as we have been approved by God to be entrusted with the gospel, even so we speak, not as pleasing men, but God who tests our hearts" (1 Thess. 2:4). In *Hell's Best Kept Secret* Ray Comfort states, "If we really believe in hell, we would plead with sinners" (Springdale, PA: Whitaker House, 1989, page 73).

17. Comfort, *Hell's Best Kept Secret*, 73.

18. "And it is the Spirit who bears witness" (1 John 5:6).

19. "Let Us make man in Our image, according to Our likeness" (Gen. 1:26). "All those who hate me love death" (Prov. 8:36). "Do I not hate them, O Lord, who hate You?" (Ps. 139:21). "If the world hates you, you know that it hated Me before it hated you" (John 15:18). Hating God or people has a demonic influence.

20. "The thief [devil] does not come except to steal, and to kill, and to destroy. I have come that they may have

life, and that they may have it more abundantly" (John 10:10). "Jesus of Nazareth...went about doing good and healing all who were oppressed by the devil" (Acts 10:38). See also Proverbs 3:2; 19:23.

21. "In My name they will cast out demons" (Mark 16:17). "Behold, I give you the authority to trample on serpents and scorpions, and over all the power of the enemy, and nothing shall by any means hurt you" (Luke 10:19). "He who is in you is greater than he who is in the world" (1 John 4:4).

22. "The love of Christ which passes knowledge" (Eph. 3:19). See also John 3:16.

23. "But for him who is joined to all the living there is hope" (Eccles. 9:4).

24. "Those who go down to the pit cannot hope for Your truth" (Isa. 38:18). "When a wicked man dies, his expectation will perish, and the hope of the unjust perishes" (Prov. 11:7). "That at that time you were without Christ...having no hope and without God in the world" (Eph. 2:12). "So are the paths of all who forget God; and the hope of the hypocrite shall perish" (Job 8:13).

25. Billy Graham, *Angels: God's Secret Agents* (Nashville: W Publishing Group, 2000), 75.

26. "Knowing, therefore, the terror of the Lord, we persuade men" (2 Cor. 5:11). "For there is one God and one mediator between God and man, the man Christ Jesus" (1 Tim. 2:5).

CHAPTER 4

THE RETURN

I LOOKED DOWN AND could see the curve of the earth.[1] It was absolutely breathtaking. As a child I was always interested in outer space. In fact, for a time I wanted to become an astronomer. Like many young boys I had always desired to see the earth from space. Now here the earth was before my eyes, so big, and it just hung there "on nothing" (Job 26:7).[2] I could feel God's power, and I knew that everything was so perfectly in His control.[3] The earth was turning so precisely, not varying even one mile per hour. The vast oceans were held within their boundaries, never spilling over onto the land, not moving past His command.[4] The earth exhibits His absolute power and control. And not only is the earth in His perfect control, but also the entire universe, with all its planets and stars, is fully in His control.[5] Yet not one sparrow "falls to the ground apart from your Father's will," and "the very hairs of your head are all numbered" (Matt. 10:29–30). The expanse of His great power is simply inconceivable.

With all that power it is a good thing that He is a good and loving God.[6] If you give most people a little earthly power, they become prideful, overconfident, and less compassionate.

Yet God has all power, and still He is love. That doesn't mean everything that happens on the earth is His will. However, it does mean that everything is within His knowledge and control. For that very reason as Christians we need to pray that "Your will be done on earth as it is in heaven" (Matt. 6:10).

As Jesus and I began moving toward the earth, the continents came into view. I remember the moment when we reentered the atmosphere. I know that reentering the earth's atmosphere is an extremely complicated ordeal for astronauts, and I sensed when we passed through that barrier.

I believe that anyone viewing the earth from space would have a difficult time denying a Creator. My parents lived near Cape Canaveral, Florida, and would host astronauts in their home on occasion. Indeed, many of them became Christians after going to space and seeing God's creation.

I was reminded of God's loving-kindness. He knows the most intimate details of our lives, yet He oversees the universe. As a child I grew up watching *Star Trek* and, as I mentioned, had always dreamed of seeing space. It is amazing to me that the Lord would remember even so small a thing as my childhood desire and allow me to experience space—with Him!

We sped toward California and quickly made our way to my home. As we hovered over the house, I could see through the roof. As I looked into the living room, I was startled to see my body lying on the living room floor.

I could hardly believe it was me. I thought, "No. This is the real me." Immediately that scripture came to mind where Paul said, "For we know that if our earthly house, *this tent*, is destroyed, we have a building from God, a house not made with hands, eternal in the heavens" (2 Cor. 5:1, emphasis added). My experience was comparable to getting out of your car, then standing back and looking at it. It's not you; it's just a vehicle to carry you around. My body lying there looked so temporal, and my life seemed so short. My life span seemed as short to me as the time it takes for steam to escape from a teakettle. It quickly vanishes away.[7] During this experience I had an understanding of eternity and a greater sense of what was important to God. Sometimes what we may think is so very important is not really important at all.

I remember passing through the roof and into my living room. As I approached my body, I seemed to be drawn back into it. It was at that time that the Lord left. Immediately the horrors of hell came back into my mind. You see, as long as the Lord was with me, the fear and torments of hell left me.[8] But when He left, the fear returned.

I started screaming and lay there in a traumatized state. I'm sure you have heard of someone in a war situation going into trauma or a car accident causing the victim severe shock. Well, hell is far worse than any horror the earth could produce. It was far beyond what anyone could bear. The human body cannot hold up under all that terror. The well-known expression "He died of fright" is entirely possible for anyone who retains the memories of hell. My cries were loud enough to reach the bedroom and wake my wife up from a deep sleep.

I will let Annette give you her perspective of that night.

ANNETTE'S STORY

I woke up to screams coming from down the hallway. My first reaction was to look to my right to see if Bill was there beside me in bed. He wasn't. I turned to my left and looked at the digital clock and noticed that it was 3:23 a.m. I got out of bed and walked down the hallway to the living room, where I found Bill in a fetal position with his hands grasping at the sides of his head. His breathing was erratic, and he was screaming, "I feel like I'm going to die!" I thought he was having a heart attack.

I asked him, "What's wrong?"

He screamed, "THE LORD TOOK ME TO HELL. PRAY FOR ME! PRAY THAT THE LORD WILL TAKE THE FEAR FROM MY MIND!"

I had never seen him this way. Bill is a reserved, calm person. All those who know him would tell you he is very even-tempered, steady, and consistent, and he has been so all his life. For Bill to be out of control and traumatized like that was completely against his nature.

It took a few seconds for me to process the shock of what I had heard. Although shocked, I felt a sense of peace inside, and I believed Bill completely. I felt a sense of relief in knowing that he wasn't having a heart attack. In my heart I knew he'd be OK. I started to pray. After a short while Bill began to calm down and regain his composure. His screaming subsided, his breathing returned to normal, and he was able to gather his thoughts. He asked me for a glass of water.

BILL'S STORY CONTINUES

I remember being amazed as I looked at the water in the glass Annette handed to me. It was life in a glass. I gulped it down and asked for another—I never wanted to be thirsty again.[9] After the second glass was finished, my wife and I returned to the bedroom. As we sat up in bed, I began to tell her what happened. I mentioned that the experience had begun at 3:00 a.m. She told me it was 3:23 a.m. when I woke her with my screams.

I had been in hell for twenty-three minutes.

After Annette prayed for me, God left the memories of my experience with me but without the horror. I'm thankful that He did. If the Lord had not taken the horror of those memories with the pain and suffering from me, I know I would have died. A person cannot live with such horror in his mind. Even natural tragedies often take years, sometimes decades, for the pain to subside to where people can look back and talk about their situations without turmoil.

I am reminded of a friend, Jake Greenwald, who is a survivor of the USS *Indianapolis*, which was sunk in the Pacific Ocean during World War II.[10] Approximately nine hundred men were left drifting in the ocean for five days without lifeboats. Approximately six hundred of the men were eaten alive by sharks. Jake has shared with me the horror that he endured as he heard the screams of his fellow crewmen during the night as they were being eaten one by one. Though he survived the sharks, the severe sunburn and salt water split Jake's back and legs open. The experience was so traumatic that it took him more than fifty years to finally talk about it.

I truly thank God that it didn't take me years, or even days, to recover from my visit to hell. In an instant God removed the fear and left the memory so I could retell the story to others.

Although I was no longer bearing the emotional distress, I was completely exhausted. The fatigue was greater than any I have ever experienced in my life.

Even so, the next day I wanted to call everyone I knew who didn't believe in hell and make him listen to me. I knew

I needed to rest and allow myself to recover, but I had to alert everyone. It wasn't just my friends and family either. I wanted to do that with everyone. In fact, it took the next year for me to settle down.

I didn't want a single person to go where I had been. I woke up each morning thinking I had to warn people, and I went to bed each night wondering whom I might have missed that day. Everywhere I went, I would look at people and think, "I wonder how many of them are going to hell.[11] I must find a way to tell them about Jesus."

During the next year there were times when I would get irritated with people who said they didn't believe in Jesus, heaven, or hell. When you know the truth, you want so desperately to convince others that hell is real and that Jesus is their only way out. Sometimes I would simply run short of patience because I knew where they were going if they didn't listen.

It is not just that I am anxious to talk to others because of my experience—it's also because of what God says in His Word. That is what counts. I do not get upset at the people themselves but at how hard it is to convince them of the truth.

To give an analogy, try to imagine how you would feel if you were sitting beside a pool and saw a tanker truck pull up with some evil-looking men in it. The men get out of the truck and begin to drain the pool water to about half full. Then they fill it back up with another liquid from the large truck. However, it's not water—it's acid! You watch the men throw a wooden board into the pool, and the board immediately disintegrates. Obviously these men are planning on killing whoever jumps into the seemingly harmless pool.

It is our bounden duty to warn sinners of their fearful
peril. To remain silent is criminal.[12] —A. W. PINK

Then the men drive away. A few minutes later some children come running up to the pool to swim. You immediately scream and warn them of the acid in the water, but they don't believe you. You desperately yell, telling them to stay out of the pool. However, the water looks great to them—it's inviting. How frustrated you would be! You couldn't let them jump in, even if they insisted. You would feel compelled to do whatever it took to save them.

I am reminded of a day when I received a call from an elderly lady who was considering selling her house. She asked me to come over to talk with her about it. She said she wanted to sell right away because she was ill.

I told her, "Why don't you wait until you're feeling a bit better and not make such a big decision while under the stress of cancer surgery?"

She then agreed to wait. In talking with her, since she seemed so close to death, I asked her if she knew Jesus. She said, "I don't believe in all that Bible fairy-tale stuff."

I tried my best to persuade her not to take a chance on her eternity. She said she thought it was all silly and told me to keep my beliefs to myself. I left with a feeling of deep sorrow. She appeared so frail and sickly that I felt she wouldn't live much longer.

The next morning she was dead. I felt such anguish for her soul. If she rejected God's last efforts due to her hardened heart, I knew she would now be in that terrible place.

It's frustrating to hear someone say, "I don't believe in that

Bible stuff. If there is a God, He would never send someone to such a horrible place." Well, *He doesn't!* He doesn't want anyone to go there—ever. He gave His life so that we might live.[13]

Here's a bit of irony. On one hand I was almost obsessed with warning people about hell and wanted to tell everyone how to avoid it. However, at the same time I didn't want to tell anyone about my personal "visit" there or about the time I spent with the Lord. Words cannot express what it was like to be in His presence. I suppose I felt somewhat like I was protecting a treasure.

For three months I kept it to myself, except for sharing it with my mother and one close friend and his wife.

CHAPTER 4 NOTES

1. "It is He who sits above the circle of the earth" (Isa. 40:22). Isaiah was written in approximately 750 BC, and yet man thought the world was flat until the time of Christopher Columbus.

2. "He made the worlds...upholding all things by the word of His power" (Heb. 1:2–3).

3. "All authority has been given to Me in heaven and on earth" (Matt. 28:18).

4. "When He assigned to the sea its limit, so that the waters would not transgress His command" (Prov. 8:29). "You have set all the borders of the earth" (Ps. 74:17).

5. "The heavens declare the glory of God; and the firmament shows His handiwork" (Ps. 19:1).

6. "God is love" (1 John 4:16).

7. "For my days are consumed like smoke" (Ps. 102:3). "What is your life? It is even a vapor that appears for a little time and then vanishes away" (James 4:14).

8. "Perfect love [which Jesus is] casts out fear" (1 John 4:18).

9. "Whoever drinks of this water will thirst again, but whoever drinks of the water that I shall give him will never thirst" (John 4:13–14). "And let him who thirsts come. Whoever desires, let him take the water of life freely" (Rev. 22:17).

10. *USS Indianapolis (CA-35) Survivors, Only 317 Survived!* (Indianapolis: Printing Partners, 2002), 183.

11. "Enter by the narrow gate; for wide is the gate and broad is the way that leads to destruction, and there are many who go in by it" (Matt. 7:13).

12. A. W. Pink, *Eternal Punishment*, Introduction, paragraph 6, accessed January 13, 2017, http://www.crta .org/eschaton/pink_eternal_punishment.html.

13. "But God demonstrates His own love toward us, in that while we were still sinners, Christ died for us. Much more then, having now been justified by His blood, we shall be saved from wrath through Him" (Rom. 5:8–9). See also Romans 6:23 and John 3:16.

[CHAPTER 5]

CONFIRMATIONS

EIGHTEEN YEARS HAVE now passed since my visit to hell, and we have not solicited at one door. But God has given us numerous opportunities to speak at dozens of churches and to share on television broadcasts and several radio broadcasts, all by invitation. I am still somewhat hesitant because I personally have never been one who enjoyed public speaking. Given the seriousness of the subject matter, it's easy to see how people could think that I either had a bad dream or that I'm just plain crazy. Either way, it's sometimes not easy to tell the whole story again.

That is not to say that I don't welcome the opportunities when they arise. They are one of the strongest confirmations to me personally that God wants this message to be heard. The e-mails, calls, and countless reports of many who have become Christians after hearing me tell my experience continue to reaffirm that God is opening the doors.

God has confirmed this experience many times. In this chapter I will share several incidents that have occurred.

A SECOND GLIMPSE

One day after the November 22, 1998, experience, I was going to drop off some business-related paperwork at a friend's home. Coincidentally this was the same house my wife and I were at the night before, just prior to my journey to hell. While driving to their home, I voiced to the Lord, "Lord, can You simply confirm that I truly was there last night? It's just so wild to think I actually went to hell. Could You show me just a glimpse of that place again for just a few seconds?"

I pulled up in front of their home and parked. Suddenly I was in hell once more. However, this time was different. During my first visit to hell I was a participant in the suffering. This time I was there only as an observer. Even so, just being there was enough to terrify me again.

This "tour" lasted no longer than ten seconds before I was back in my car, trying to deal with what had happened, now for the second time. It took me a good twenty minutes, sitting alone in my car, to calm down and gather myself to where I could conduct the business I needed to conduct. The shock stayed with me as I entered the home and barely spoke a word. At one point my friend asked, "Are you all right?"

I simply replied, "Oh, I'm fine, thank you," then finished my business and left.

As I was driving home, my first thought was that I needed to tell my wife what had happened. I realized, "This is pretty serious." I was stunned by what I had seen but also grateful that the Lord had so quickly answered my prayer and confirmed the experience so concretely. However, I had had enough of that place. I asked the Lord to never, ever take me back there. To this day He hasn't.

A DIVINE INTERRUPTION

One week later I was having lunch with three local pastors. As we were sitting in the restaurant having light conversation, one of the pastors mentioned having some repair work done on his car. Out of the blue he abruptly changed the subject matter and turned to me and said, "Can you imagine how horrible it must be for people in hell? It must be so awful. We must warn people." Then, just as abruptly, he turned to the other pastors and continued to discuss his car repairs. It was as if he and the other pastors didn't even notice what was said. It was really strange since all of them were unaware of my experience at this point. It was as if God was using him to speak to me.

No more than three months later my wife and I were with this same group of pastors. The same pastor who spoke to me of hell at that earlier lunch now felt compelled to say, "Bill, I sense that you have been through something traumatic. You should tell us about it." It wasn't until then that I shared the experience with them.

A DIVINE CONNECTION

I had not wanted to tell anyone what had happened, and I did not for three weeks. My wife and I were at lunch with a couple with whom we are friends, and my wife felt that I should share my experience with them. After I had told them, they mentioned a certain book by a woman who had also seen hell and asked if we had read it. We told them we had not. They said that in her book this woman told of some of the same experiences I had talked about. We purchased the book and couldn't put it down. We wanted to meet the author, but we did not know how to contact her personally, much less set up a meeting.

About two weeks later I was on the phone with my mom, planning a trip to visit. During our conversation she told me how she had recently listened to a tape by a woman who gave her testimony about a visit to hell. It turned out to be the very woman whose book we had just read. So I proceeded to tell my mom what had happened to me. After a few more days my mother called me back. She had discovered that she and this woman attended the same church.

When we arrived for our visit, we discovered that this woman had arrived back in town the same day. And when we attended church on Sunday, she did too. This, in itself, was a miracle because her speaking schedule keeps her busy throughout the world and doesn't allow her to attend many services per year. After the service we got the chance to meet her, and we talked for about three hours. It helped me immensely to be able to talk with someone else who had been there.

She was able to tell me some of the things she went through after her experience, and this helped prepare me for what I encountered. She knew just what I was going through, and she was able to explain many of my feelings. Over the next few months there were times when I would find myself in circumstances or feeling a certain way, and her generous words would come to my memory and help me through whatever I was facing. I truly believe it was no accident that I was able to meet her.

A GENTLE GIANT

When in hell I had only thought specifically of three people: my wife, my friend Pastor Raul, and someone we didn't know personally but had seen frequently at the gym. This third man did not know us, but you couldn't miss him when he was around because of how massive and powerfully built he was. I remember thinking of him as I was being held down by some of the demons in hell. He came to my mind as I thought, "Even the strongest guy I've seen would be no match for these creatures."

About two weeks after my experience my wife and I were at the gym, riding stationary bikes, when the huge man walked past us. He suddenly stopped and said, "Do you mind if I ask you a question?"

We said no, that we wouldn't mind, so he asked, "Do you know anything about God?"

"Yes," we replied.

"I know this might sound weird," he continued, "but I feel like God is calling me. I just had this feeling that I should stop and talk to you."

We talked with him at length, and we became friends. After time he also received Jesus as his Savior. As we got to know him, I discovered that he had won a regional Strongest Man contest in 1996, and he's still one of the biggest men I have ever seen.

CHURCH LEADERS LISTEN

Three months after my experience I called a close friend of twenty-five years, Darrel Ballman, and his wife, Evie, to confide in them. They are two of the most mature and seasoned Christians I know. Darrel has always been a respected church leader and very knowledgeable in biblical matters. After I told them my story, they asked me to speak to approximately fifty church leaders and pastors they would invite to their home. It turned out to be a great meeting. Everyone there felt that the experience was genuine and appreciated what I had shared.

One of the pastors talked to us afterward. He told us he had been praying recently and felt that he was going to be learning more about hell in the near future. He thought that God was going to reveal some truths about hell to him and that he was to share them with his congregation. This had been published in his church's newsletter. A few weeks later he felt a desire to call a friend of his named Darrel. He didn't have a particular reason to call him but felt that he should. In their phone conversation Darrel mentioned that he was going to have a man come to his house and speak of his recent journey to hell. Immediately this minister spoke up and said, "That's it! I'm supposed to be there." So he came. After hearing our testimony and speaking with us afterward, he was convinced that my wife and I were to visit his church. In fact, many of the other leaders also asked us to speak to their church or Bible study. We accepted each invitation and witnessed God's love draw many to Christ.

AN ANSWER TO A PRAYER

Another time my wife and I were asked to speak at a large Russian church in Sacramento, California. We went, and it turned out to be a marvelous experience, one we will never forget. It was a very orthodox but Spirit-filled church. The women still wore the shawls over their heads and dresses down to their ankles. Many had escaped Russia and had been in the concentration camps in Germany during the 1940s.

After speaking that evening, one of the elders of the church came up to us and told us through an interpreter that he was a Russian Jew and had been thrown into the ovens at one of the prisoner camps. A friend had pulled him out of the oven and was able to bring him back to life. He said that during that experience he had died and had been taken to hell. He told me he had seen exactly what I had shared with the group that night.

With tears streaming down his weathered face, he said he had prayed that one day someone would come and confirm what he had seen. Finally, after fifty-six years, his prayer was answered. He had written a book about his experience, which he signed and gave to us. He thanked us so much for coming and answering his prayer for all those years. Knowing that we had been an answer to that old man's prayers after all those years left us with a feeling of great honor and humility.

The next night I was asked to speak on the Russian TV broadcast that would air in Sacramento and Los Angeles, California; Canada; and Russia. This old gentleman came out to the TV station and sat in the front row to honor and encourage us. We appreciated that very much. The Russian people, especially those who head up the TV ministry, were exceptional people. They were so dedicated to serving the Lord. We really liked them and have remained in contact with them. They were so grateful to be in America and to have all the freedoms that we take for granted. We knew we were in God's perfect will in going on that trip.

A COLLEGE CLASSROOM

I was being interviewed on a radio program with Holly McClure, and an e-mail came in from a professor at a college in Southern California. This was a public college, not a Christian school. The professor asked if I would share my experience with his philosophy class, as the class was discussing life-after-death issues. My wife and I went, and we found it to be another "being in God's will" experience.

I had not gotten five minutes into the story when there were hands flying into the air with questions—very good questions. The students were so unfamiliar with the things of God, but they were eager to learn and get answers. They wanted to know many things: "Why would there be such a place as hell?" "Why would God send anyone there?" "How do you know this wasn't just your own preconceived and learned ideas that caused you to perhaps just dream up such a thing?" "How can one be good enough, then, to go to heaven?" "Don't you have to work your way to salvation?" and so on.

We were able to clear up numerous questions for these young people. Most of the students had never read a Bible or been exposed to church. Very few of them had ever seen the *Ten Commandments* movie or any other religious films. So many of today's young people are taught that whatever seems right to them is OK. They are not told that there is a definite right and wrong, and they know nothing about God's great love for them and His will for their lives.

It's very interesting to see how young people react to this story. To be honest, I'm not the type of person to whom they would naturally be drawn. There are many who are more dynamic, more exciting, more charismatic, who would seem to better fit the part. But I think that's just another confirmation that God is behind this message.

Normally younger people have a short attention span and need constant entertainment if you want to hold their interest. Nevertheless, almost every opportunity I have had to speak to that generation has been very fruitful. They always seem to listen intently and absorb every word.

RADIO CALL

After a radio interview with Holly McClure a woman called in. She said she was driving down the road with her teenage son, and he was listening to some awful, headbanger music. She told him she couldn't stand hearing it any longer and tried changing the station. He kept changing it back to his music. She changed it again, this time to Holly's interview with me. The son listened for approximately fifteen seconds and then told his mother to keep it there. She was shocked. He listened to the entire program and told her he needed to accept the Lord. He didn't want to go to hell. She was amazed, as she had tried for so long to get through to him. She called to thank Holly for having me on the air.

THE YOUNGER GENERATION

I'll never forget when my wife and I were invited to a pastor's home in the Anaheim Hills area of Southern California. This home had a very large rear yard, and to our amazement the house was set up with a full stage, a screen, and professional lighting. Approximately two hundred high school students came that evening to hear some Christian musicians and, afterward, my account of hell. They really put forth a tremendous effort, and it was wonderful to see so many young people dedicate and rededicate their lives to Christ.

Another time I was invited to address a youth ministry in south Orange County. You could hear a pin drop as I shared my experience with the youths. They listened with such intent, had a lot of questions, and desperately wanted material to share with their friends. After I spoke with them, the youth pastor told me he had never seen them so attentive before.

It is a privilege to speak before the younger generation. They are sharp, are smart, and don't cut you any slack. I appreciate their directness and their inquisitiveness regarding God and the supernatural.

KANSAS CITY

This is another account of God's orchestrating and providing confirmation. We were at a prayer meeting one night, and a pastor said, "I feel you are to go to Kansas City, that God is doing something big in Kansas." The next day we received a call from Hal Linhardt, a longtime pastor in the Kansas City area, who asked if we would come out to speak at several churches. He had seen a video of my wife and me, and he really wanted us to come out and share. We knew that God was telling us to go.

After we arrived in Kansas, Hal told us how all this came about. He had recently joined forces with another ministry. A lady close to the ministry had a vision of hell and was very disturbed by it. She told the pastor about the vision, and it prompted him to ask Hal for an in-depth study on hell. During Hal's study another leader of the church said he had seen a video of us sharing our experience about hell. He gave the video to Hal, who knew this was a sign from God to help him complete his study. He asked his pastor if he could invite me to speak at their church. His pastor agreed, so he contacted us.

We were delighted to get to know him and his family during our week in Kansas City. Though we were there for only a short visit, we felt we had become lifelong friends. We were inspired by his humble attitude, his excellent character, his stand for truth, and his dedication to Jesus. During that week we spoke at five different churches. At each one we saw people respond to the message. People of all ages shared with us that God had touched their hearts through our words and that their lives were changed.

One particular teenager came forward and gave his life to Jesus. Just one week earlier he had tried to commit suicide because he faced jail time for a recent car accident.

Another person I remember was a little seven-year-old girl. She and her mother came up to us after one of the meetings. It was clear that she had been crying, and her mother proceeded to tell us of how strongly her daughter was affected by our story. Her daughter had told her, "We have to tell our neighbors about Jesus because they are going to hell!" She was so upset that she was sobbing at the thought of her neighbors perishing in such a horrible place. Her mother was touched by her daughter's sincerity and compassion for others, and she thanked us for coming and sharing the story with the church. We were deeply moved and humbled by the reaction of this little girl and her commitment to do something to help her neighbors.

At another church on this trip we met a lady who was concerned for her husband. For years she had tried to get him to go to church with her, but he consistently resisted. After the meeting she approached us and asked where we would be speaking next. She thought the story was unusual enough to get her husband's attention and that he might be willing to hear us. Sure enough, she showed up with her husband the very next morning at the last church on that trip.

Afterward she came up to us again and introduced us to her husband. We weren't sure what to expect, as he was not a regular churchgoer. To our surprise he was excited and glad he had come. He told us he thought most churches were filled with hypocritical rhetoric and that he didn't need to attend, but now he had a different outlook altogether. "I want to thank you for opening my eyes," he said. He could see that he had misjudged both God and the Bible and was choosing to believe differently in the future. He was completely changed, and his wife seemed eternally grateful. "If you're ever back in town, you can stay with us!" they said.

These are just a few of the numerous experiences in Kansas City that really touched us. Several years have passed since our visit to Kansas City, but the reports continue to pour in via e-mail of many coming to Christ after hearing about the reality of hell.

AROUND THE WORLD

Our first venture out of the state was to a little church in Texas. Although there were only about a hundred people there, the meeting turned out to have a far greater effect than we could have imagined. We didn't know it at the time, but the church had videotaped the meeting.

Even though the tape didn't turn out to be the most professional quality, it has literally reached the world. We have had reports from all across America and many other nations, including China, Japan, Australia, and New Zealand. Many calls and e-mails have come in, all with positive reports.

The tape had not been advertised, marketed, or distributed in any formal way. This grassroots distribution is something we never could have foreseen or planned. I truly believe it has been orchestrated by God to get the message out. In fact, a similar thing has happened with an audio CD of this message.

Later, Hal was in a meeting, telling the story of my trip to hell. One of the men in the audience happened to own an audio duplicating company and said he felt this message needed to be spread. He offered to duplicate fifteen hundred CDs for free to be handed out in their community. Several churches in the area got excited and decided to pass the CDs out on Halloween. They have done this for the past three years now; they have distributed more than seven thousand CDs in the Kansas City area alone.

MORE RADIO

Recently I received a phone call from a Christian radio talk-show host. He had heard a tape of my account, and it had so impacted him that he wanted to interview me. As we talked, he shared his near-death experience. He died and was on his way to hell, but he had been revived. He said that he had traveled down a large tunnel-like cavern. This cavern was lined with evil creatures of every shape and size. The creatures desperately tried to grab him as he descended. As the light continually decreased, the fear inside him grew steadily stronger. He knew he was on his way to hell.

He said he knew I was telling the truth. Besides, he

appreciated all of the Scripture references I gave to vali-
date the experience. The radio show was a success, and he
expressed a desire to have me on the air again.

FOUND IN A RENTAL CAR

This story is inspiring. There is a gentleman who works at a
rental car agency in Kansas City as a service agent. One day
he found a CD on the ground in his service bay. It had been
removed from one of the rental cars and was headed for a
trash can since there was no way to identify which car it came
from. The CD was titled "23 Minutes in Hell." This service
agent was intrigued by the title and thought he'd listen to
it. He said that for the next forty minutes or so, he couldn't
turn it off. He admitted that he had really never thought
much about religion and had never been a churchgoer. He
said he had pretty good radar for someone not telling the
truth, as he had lied a lot in his day. He thought, "This guy
either really believes he was in hell, or he was actually there."
He couldn't think of anything else the rest of the night, and
at the end of the CD he prayed.

JUST IN TIME

This last story is quite sobering. It reminds us that life is
truly short, and some decisions should be made quickly.

I received an e-mail from a lady in Georgia. As a boy
her son gave his life to God and was living a good life.
Unfortunately during his teen years his life took a bad turn,
and he got involved with drugs and alcohol. He began to
get into trouble and was in and out of jails and hospitals for
twenty years. One night in June 2005 his mother was listening to the CD "23 Minutes in Hell," which tells the story

that's in this book. To her surprise her son stopped to listen and took the message seriously. At the end of the CD there is a prayer, and her son repeated it. He was so excited! He told his mother that he was going to church with her the following Sunday to tell of how he'd been changed, but he never made it. He died in his sleep that night at age thirty-nine. In his mother's e-mail she said, "Amidst our grief at losing Brian so suddenly, we have the joy of knowing he is in the presence of the Lord Jesus." One day more would have been too late, but God's mercy spared him an eternity of torment.

There have been many other confirmations. I could go on with story after story. We have not sought out one opportunity, but God continues to open up doors to share this message.

There are no words that are descriptive enough or adequate to truly allow you to imagine such a nightmare. It is my sincere hope that in the pages of this book I have been able to convey the reality of the agony one will go through in hell. Please take this seriously. I strongly urge you to read all the scriptures for yourself.

> But God demonstrates His own love toward us, in that while we were still sinners, Christ died for us. Much more then, having now been justified by His blood, we shall be saved from wrath through Him.
>
> —ROMANS 5:8–9

CHAPTER 6

CAN "GOOD" PEOPLE GO TO HELL?

Yᴏᴜ ᴍɪɢʜᴛ ʙᴇ thinking, "Am I a good enough person to go to heaven? Yes, I think I am. Who goes to hell? Only bad people—really bad people, such as Hitler, Stalin, murderers, rapists, and so forth. People who kill little children. Those are the really bad people."

This sounds reasonable to most of us. But what standard is used to determine if one is "good enough" to go to heaven and another is "bad enough" to go to hell? What criterion determines our eternal fate? Could it be based on a higher standard? This is something we all need to know for certain. What authority can give us those answers?

The Bible has much to say about this widely misunderstood subject. Perhaps you even have your own opinion about the realities of hell. Are you willing to risk your eternity on "your opinion"? Since the Bible has undergone such intense scrutiny, thorough investigation, and thousands of years of testing, you may want to at least research what it has to say about this matter.

The qualification for entrance into heaven (or hell) is not

based on how we compare with others. You may look pretty good to yourself, but what if you were looked at through the eyes of one who is sinless? What if you were judged not only by your actions but also by your thoughts? Would that make you a little more uncomfortable? If we are honest, we will admit that our actions alone would condemn us.

A girl was looking at a beautiful hillside covered with lush, green grass. She noticed a herd of sheep standing on the hill. They looked so white and clean, especially against the dark green grass. The girl went to bed, and the next morning she walked outside to look at the sheep. However, it had snowed all night. The sheep were still there, but now, against the unblemished white snow, they looked dingy, even dirty.[1] In the same way, our "goodness" when compared with God's standard for "good" falls far, far short.

Or perhaps you view your actions and thoughts in the same way Danny viewed his parking tickets. Ray Comfort, in his book *How to Live Forever...Without Being Religious*, explains what happened to his friend Danny:

> When he told me that he once went to prison for failing to pay parking tickets, I asked, "Why didn't you just pay them?" He answered, "They were just parking tickets; it was no big deal." Then he told me that the police arrived at his home at 4:00 a.m., put him in a big black bus, and took him to Los Angeles County court. As he stood before the judge, he said, "Your Honor, I brought $700 with me to pay the tickets and to cover the court costs." The judge said, "Mr. Goodall, I'm going to save you all that money. You are going to jail!"[2]

Danny was terrified.

His big mistake was that he trivialized his crimes by thinking they were "just" parking tickets, and so he deceived himself. Had he known the judge's ruling (that he would go to prison), he would have immediately made things right between himself and the law.

Most of us realize that we have broken God's law—the Ten Commandments—but it's no big deal. So let me ask you a few questions about the law you have broken and see if it is a big deal. Have you ever lied? You say, "Yes. But they were only white lies. They were nothing serious." Have you ever stolen something? You say, "Yes, but only little things." Can you see what you are doing? You are trivializing your crimes, and, like Danny, you will deceive yourself. What you are doing is saying you haven't actually "sinned," and the Bible warns, "If we say that we have no sin, we deceive ourselves" (1 John 1:8–9). The truth is, if you have lied, then you are a liar. If you have stolen anything (the value of the item stolen is irrelevant), you are a thief.

What you need to hear is the judge's ruling for lying and stealing. Here it is: "All liars shall have their part in the lake which burns with fire and brimstone" (Rev. 21:8). All liars go to hell. You say, "I don't believe in hell." That's like someone saying to the judge, "I don't believe in jail." What we believe or don't believe doesn't change reality. No thief will enter heaven. Not one.[3] Now look at this: Jesus said, "Whoever looks at a woman to lust for her has already committed adultery with her in his heart" (Matt. 5:28). Have you ever looked with lust? Then you have committed adultery, as far as God is concerned. Have you used God's name in vain? If you have, then you have used His holy name as a cuss word to express disgust. That's called blasphemy, and it's very serious in God's sight.

So if you have been honest enough to admit that you have broken those commandments, you are a self-admitted lying, thieving, blasphemous adulterer at heart. If God gives you justice on Judgment Day, you will be guilty and end up in hell. Think of it—if you died right now, you would end up in hell forever. So what are you going to do? How can you make things right between you and the law? The Bible tells us that you cannot "do" anything.[4] Further, keep in mind that a good judge must carry out justice.

There was a judge in a town that had a case brought to him one day. A girl was speeding in her car through an intersection that had signs posted warning drivers to drive slowly and watch for blind, handicapped children crossing the street. A police officer stopped her vehicle and gave her a ticket. The judge set the fine at the maximum—$25,000. Since the girl was unable to pay the fine, the bailiff prepared to take her away to jail. Just then, the judge did something very strange. He got up from his bench, went over to the bailiff, and paid the $25,000 for her! People wondered what was going on; only later did they find out that the girl was his daughter. Even though it was his daughter, the judge still imposed the maximum fine. He had to carry out justice. However, his love for his daughter would not allow him to leave her in that predicament.[5]

In just the same manner God did not leave us in a hopeless state concerning our eternity. Just as the judge paid the fine for his daughter, so likewise Jesus paid the penalty for all of our sins. He was brutally beaten beyond recognition as a man, He was severely whipped, and He was nailed to a cross, where He suffered an excruciating death. He paid the fine in His life's blood for the crimes that you committed: "God demonstrates His own love toward us, in that while we were still sinners, Christ died for us" (Rom. 5:8). Then He rose from the dead and defeated death.

Ray continues:

> Now here's the difference between being religious and being a Christian. There are millions of people on this earth who have never seen the serious nature of sin. They are in the dark about the judge's ruling. They have no idea that they will end up in hell for crimes that they consider trivial. They know that they have to face God after death, but they think that their religious works (like Danny with his $700) will buy their way out of any trouble in which they may find themselves. And as long as they trivialize their sin, they will deceive themselves into thinking that they can work their way into heaven by their religious works. But it is as futile as the man who tried to row against the river until he went over the falls. God Himself has thrown us a rope in Jesus Christ. He is the only One that can save us from death and hell. But we must let go of our own efforts to save ourselves and take hold of the rope. The moment we cease our own religious "rowing" and have faith in Jesus, that's when we find peace with God.[6]

The Bible says, "For by grace you have been saved through faith, and that not of yourselves; it is the gift of God, not of works, lest anyone should boast" (Eph. 2:8–9).

You still may wonder how a good and loving God could send someone to that horrific place called hell. To put it plainly, He doesn't. It is your rejection of the provision (Jesus) for your sin that sends you there. We all have a free will, and we can choose not to repent. (*Repent* means "to turn or change.") In Deuteronomy 30:19 God says, "I have set before you life and death, blessing and cursing; therefore *choose life*" (emphasis added). Jesus said, "I am the way, the truth, and the life. No one comes to the Father except through Me" (John 14:6). Will you believe Jesus? Or will you reject Him?

By choosing to do nothing, you have already made a choice. You choose death and hell forever. There are no "fence" positions. In John 3:18 Jesus says, "He who believes in Him is not condemned; but he who does not believe is condemned already, because he has not believed in the name of the only begotten Son of God." I am horrified at the thought of anyone spending an eternity in hell. Please don't take this lightly, but believe what the Bible has to say. It is your eternity you are dealing with.

Some may think that they have done too many things wrong and that God could not forgive them. The Bible clearly says that God has plenty of mercy for everyone. Psalm 86:5 says, "For You, Lord, are good, and ready to forgive, and abundant in mercy to all those who call upon You." He will forgive all of your sins the moment you ask, and He will remember them no more.[7] To receive Jesus as your Savior, please pray something like this:

> *Dear God, I confess I am a sinner. Thank You that Jesus took my punishment upon Himself when He died on the cross for my sins, and then rose from*

the dead, defeating death. Today I repent and place my trust in Jesus Christ alone for my salvation. In Jesus's name I pray. Amen.

If you have prayed this short prayer, then you have made the wisest decision you will ever make. Begin reading your Bible, starting with the Gospel of John. Find a Bible-believing church to attend, and go and tell someone what you have done, as Jesus said to do in Matthew 10:32. Pursue Him, and you will fulfill your purpose in life.

CHAPTER 6 NOTES

1. Comfort, *Hell's Best Kept Secret*, 113.

2. The story of Danny is adapted from Ray Comfort, *How to Live Forever...Without Being Religious* (N.p: n.d.).

3. "Nor thieves...will inherit the kingdom of God" (1 Cor. 6:10).

4. Comfort, *How to Live Forever...Without Being Religious*.

5. Josh McDowell, *More Than a Carpenter* (Wheaton, IL: Tyndale House, 1977), 115.

6. Comfort, *How to Live Forever...Without Being Religious*.

7. "For I will be merciful to their unrighteousness, and their sins and their lawless deeds I will remember no more" (Heb. 8:12).

Annette describes how she first found Bill lying on their living room floor after his return from this life-changing experience.

During this weekend of ministry at Free Chapel in Gainesville, Georgia, approximately five hundred people came to Christ.

At Free Chapel in Gainesville, Georgia, an excited congregation of thousands welcomes Bill and the message of *23 Minutes in Hell*. The enthusiasm of this body of believers is palpable every time he is invited to speak.

Pastor Jentezen Franklin and Bill lead hundreds of people in the prayer of salvation at Free Chapel's Irvine, California, campus.

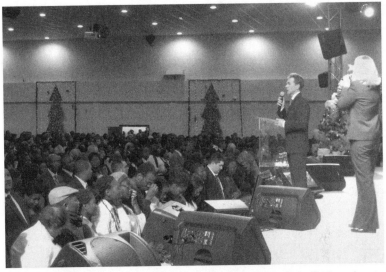

Eight hundred people receive Christ at Charisma church in Paris.

The House Modesto in California hosts a weeklong soul-winning event each year, which culminates with Bill's ministering the message of *23 Minutes in Hell*. On this occasion five hundred people gave their hearts to Christ.

Bill ministers to open hearts at Fire and Water International Church in Phoenix, Arizona. God's Spirit continues to radically transform lives at this inner-city church.

Bill ministers from Trinity Broadcasting Network in Orlando, Florida. A record number of people prayed to receive Christ that evening as a result of the broadcast.

Bill is always welcomed by an exuberant crowd at The Rock church in Anaheim, California. Fruit abounds as over five hundred people eagerly respond to his testimony.

Over one thousand people stream forward to receive Christ at Family Christian Center in Munster, Indiana.

With over one hundred thousand people in attendance at the outdoor LifeLight Festival in Sioux Falls, South Dakota, God arrests the crowd's attention as Bill ministers to his largest audience ever. Approximately five thousand people responded to the invitation to receive Jesus Christ.

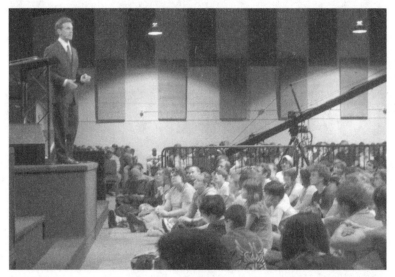

At the International House of Prayer in Kansas City, Missouri, Bill shares with an attentive audience of over two thousand, many of them young adults.

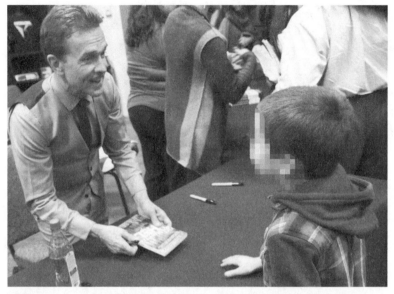

This boy was eager to talk to Bill at the book signing table. Bill enjoys every opportunity to encourage and speak into the next generation.

Bill ministers to thousands at Christian Family Church in Johannesburg, Africa, and one thousand people commit to following Christ. Ten percent of those new Christians attended and completed Bible school. All one hundred of them went into full-time ministry and missions.

PART II

RESEARCH AFTER THE RETURN: QUESTIONS AND ANSWERS ABOUT HELL

AFTER RETURNING FROM my experience of hell, I wanted to know what the Bible has to say about this subject. I recognized that my salvation would allow me to avoid this place of fire when I die, but other than that I really knew very little. I had been a Christian for twenty-eight years, but I had never studied that area of Scripture. One thing I was sure of: if what I experienced was true, then I should be able to find proof of it in the Bible.

To my surprise I discovered that there are approximately 150 verses that reveal some aspect of hell, together confirming everything I had experienced. I had no idea that the Bible included so many descriptions about this place. A few verses would have been welcome, but finding this many was overwhelming! The Bible tells us not to add to or take away anything from His Word, so it was very settling to have such solid confirmation.[1] What is really important for us to understand is what the Bible has to say about this, not my personal experience. (See Acts 17:11.)

So my wife and I began researching the verses, as well as reading scholastically respected books on the subject and receiving information from others who have had an experience with hell. I have also acquired many teachings from a vast array of scholars who have spoken on the subject. That is not to say that I am now an "expert" on the subject of hell. I readily admit that I am not, nor am I a scholar or a theologian. However, you do not need to be a scholar to read and understand the Bible. It is written for the common man. I will attempt to address the issues in regard to the events I experienced in light of the Scriptures.

You might be thinking that the Bible can be interpreted many different ways, but that's really not the case. If you are properly informed, the Bible is very clear in all that it has to say.

Why, then, does the Bible seem so controversial? Why does the truth seem so difficult to find? Most of the apostles were killed for speaking and writing the truth. Pascal, a French philosopher, said, "I prefer to believe those writers who get their throats cut for what they write."[2] Pontius Pilate, the Roman procurator, even asked Jesus, "What is truth?" (John 18:38). The truth allures men, yet it eludes them also. One reason is because many are quick to condemn before they investigate. Solomon, the wisest man who ever lived (excluding Jesus), said it this way: "He who answers a matter before he hears it, it is folly and shame to him" (Prov. 18:13). If we set aside our own opinions and seek true understanding, then we become the beneficiaries.

The main reason why truth is difficult to find is because the acceptance of truth is hindered by man's pride and arrogance. All of us possess some knowledge, but none of us can know it all. Chuck Missler, an exceptional scholar with a genius IQ, has said, "The only sure barrier to truth is to assume you already have it."[3] Our nature is to get defensive when told we're wrong, and it is this stubborn unwillingness to receive instruction and/or correction that keeps truth from us. Billy Graham said, "The sin of pride particularly has caused the downfall of Lucifer in heaven; most certainly it can bring mortal man down too."[4] He sums it up by saying, "He [Satan] forever tries to discredit the truthfulness of the Word of God; he coaxes men to deny the authority of God, and persuades the world to wallow in the deluding comforts of sin."[5] If we can lay aside our presumptions and presuppositions, perhaps the misconceptions we have can be repudiated. The fact is, *truth* is found in the pages of the Bible. But there are many who do not want to recognize God's Word as truth because of the light it sheds on our sin. Jesus Himself tells us plainly what truth is. He said, "I am the way, the truth, and the life" (John 14:6).

My desire to uncover the truth about hell caused me to draw from many sources in my research. In doing so, I was able to address some of the questions that many have asked about hell. This section of the book contains many of these questions. With each question chapter, I will quote key biblical references, along with comments from respected leaders and my own personal thoughts. If you are interested, you can refer to Appendix A for an additional list of scriptures that I believe pertain to hell, and to Appendix B, which contains some additional comments from the "Hall of Fame."

PART II NOTES

1. See Deuteronomy 12:32; Proverbs 30:6; Revelation 22:18–19.

2. Pascal (1623–1662), French philosopher and mathematician who developed the modern theory of probability, "The Bible—Quotes From Famous Men," Why-the-Bible.com, accessed January 15, 2017, http://www .why-the-bible.com/bible.htm.

3. Chuck Missler, "Return of the Nephilim," 66/40 Radio Broadcast with Chuck Missler, available as an audio CD, VHS videocassette, or DVD from Koinonia House.

4. Graham, *Angels: God's Secret Agents*, 103.

5. Ibid., 106.

CHAPTER 7

WHAT YOU BELIEVE IS IMPORTANT

WHY SHOULD YOU BELIEVE ME?

I can appreciate and understand why you might be skeptical in regard to my experience. I know I would be. I came from a conservative background where I received sound biblical teaching from conservative Bible teachers who would probably shun my experience. These learned PhDs and college professors would agree that hell exists and would not have a problem with most of the scriptures contained in Appendix A.

However, it is very likely that many of them would have an incredulous opinion about God's taking someone there for an experience such as the one I had. And I would agree, for I too have been skeptical of such "experiences" in the past. Yet the fact remains that this did occur to me, and Scripture supports that such an experience could take place.

In looking back, it took nearly a year for me to settle down from the effects of this experience. A bad dream or even a nightmare would not nearly have the same effect on someone. I was completely traumatized after the return, and only the Lord, through the prayer of my wife, brought me out of it. My life will never be the same in terms of how I view anyone who does not know Him. I will do all I can to share the truth with others.

If you choose not to believe me, it really doesn't matter. It is not my experience that is important for you to believe but what the Word of God has to say about the matter. I sincerely hope my experience will cause you to investigate the Scriptures for yourself.

WHY SHOULD YOU BELIEVE THE BIBLE?

Many people go through life never taking the time to investigate what the Bible has to say. Some think it is simply a collection of quaint stories and colorful metaphors. Others will say, "It is a good history book but has no relevance to my life." Still others believe it is written for people who, in the past, were simple-minded, or they believe that the Bible is no longer relevant in our modern society.

People will usually believe whatever religious beliefs they were raised with and not question them. They adhere to that old saying "Never discuss religion or politics," thereby remaining uninformed on the subject. It is not my intent to disparage another's beliefs but rather to extend to them facts to which they may not have had exposure. Dr. Chuck Missler said, "One of the penalties of our casual or reluctant attitude about death and dying is that most people are steeped in myths and misconceptions. Almost every commonly held belief is erroneous, misleading, and contrary to what we do know about the subject."[1]

Many of us make plans for our retirement years to enjoy a secure future. If a trip to Europe is planned, we investigate thoroughly before departure—yet we pay little or no attention to our eternity. Why are so many willing to gamble with something of such significance and about which they have so little information?

I have known the Lord and lived by His Word for more than thirty-five years. In all that time He has always provided for my needs, has helped me avoid many of life's difficulties, and has resolved every problem I encountered. If I told you how blessed I have been, you would probably think that I was either exaggerating or boasting or was perhaps delusional. So I will refrain from such remarks. The point is this: if you live by His Word, He is faithful to keep His promises. I say this with all seriousness.

You might say, "Why put such importance on the Bible? Isn't it just a book written by men? Men make mistakes." The Bible is far more unique than any other book written. It has been scrutinized by an endless array of scholars, historians, archaeologists, scientists, mathematicians, and the like for thousands of years. There have not been any discrepancies or errors that could not be cleared up with good scholarship. In the following paragraphs I have included a representative sampling of such credible scholarship.

Dr. John Warwick Montgomery, a well-known Bible scholar, has said: "I myself have never encountered an alleged contradiction in the Bible which could not be cleared up by the use of the original language of the Scriptures and/or by the use of accepted principles of literary and historical interpretation."[2] Dr. Montgomery is an extremely qualified scholar, holds two doctorates and seven undergraduate degrees, has written forty books and one hundred twenty-five journals, and is a founding member of the World Association of Law Professors.

Dr. Gleason L. Archer said:

> I candidly believe I have been confronted with just about all the biblical difficulties under discussion in theological circles today...as I have dealt with one apparent discrepancy after another....My confidence in the trustworthiness of the Scripture has been repeatedly verified and strengthened by the discovery that almost every problem in Scripture that has been discovered by man, from ancient times until now, has been dealt with in a completely satisfactory manner by the biblical text itself.[3]

Dr. Archer holds a bachelor of divinity from Princeton and a doctorate from Harvard Graduate School, has a full law degree, speaks fifteen languages, and has done extensive studies in archaeology, among other things.

Dr. Robert Dick Wilson said, "I have made it an invariable habit never to accept an objection to a statement of the Old Testament without subjecting it to a most thorough investigation, linguistically and factually."[4] He holds a doctorate from Princeton and is the author of *A Scientific Investigation of the Old Testament.*[5] Without missing a single syllable, he can repeat from memory the entire New Testament in Hebrew and can do the same with large portions of the Old Testament. He speaks forty-five languages.

Henry M. Morris, PhD, a respected scientist, points out, "It must be extremely significant that, in view of the great mass of corroborative evidence regarding the biblical history of these periods, there exists today not one unquestionable find of archeology that proves the Bible to be in error at any point."[6]

If you still are unsure about the credibility of the Bible as God's Word, I encourage you to look in the bibliography for some recommended books.

Many of the Founding Fathers of this great country believed in the absolute truth of God's Word. Here is a sampling of their comments:

> You do well to wish to learn our arts and way of life, and above all, the religion of Jesus Christ....Congress will do everything they can to assist you in this wise intention.[7]
>
> —GEORGE WASHINGTON

> The first and almost the only book deserving of universal attention is the Bible.[8]
>
> —JOHN QUINCY ADAMS

> History will also afford frequent opportunities of showing the necessity of a public religion...and the excellency of the Christian religion above all others, ancient or modern.[9]
>
> —BENJAMIN FRANKLIN

> [The Bible] is a book worth more than all the other books that were ever printed.[10]
>
> —PATRICK HENRY

> Bibles are strong entrenchments. Where they abound, men cannot pursue wicked courses.[11]
>
> —JAMES MCHENRY,
> SIGNER OF THE CONSTITUTION

> The Bible...is the one supreme source of revela-
> tion of the meaning of life, the nature of God
> and spiritual nature and need of men. It is the
> only guide of life which really leads the spirit in
> the way of peace and salvation.[12]
>
> —WOODROW WILSON

The Bible is not just *a* book but a collection of sixty-six books written by at least forty authors over approximately a fifteen-hundred-year period. The authors were historians, military generals, prophets, kings, politicians, a doctor, a rabbi, fishermen, and even a tax collector. It was written on three continents and in three different languages: Hebrew, Greek, and Aramaic.[13] They all wrote about the coming Savior. Every word was inspired by God.[14] The famous poet Voltaire said that within one hundred years of his time Christianity would be "swept from existence and passed into history." Yet fifty years after his death the Geneva Bible Society used his house and printing press to produce stacks of Bibles.[15] Jesus Himself made this statement: "My words will by no means pass away" (Mark 13:31). Dr. H. L. Hastings, a well-known writer, is cited saying, "If this book had not been the book of God, men would have destroyed it long ago. Emperors and popes, kings and priests, princes and rulers have all tried their hand at it; they die and the book still lives."[16]

There are more than three hundred prophecies in the Old Testament in regard to the birth, life, death, and resurrection of Jesus. No other book has been written foretelling the future with such accuracy. Professor Wilber Smith, DD, who taught at Fuller Theological Seminary and Trinity Evangelical Divinity School, said:

> Not in the entire gamut of Greek and Latin lit-
> erature...can we find any real specific prophecy
> of a great historic event to come in the distant
> future, nor any prophecy of a Savior to arise in
> the human race...neither can the founders of any
> cult in this country rightly identify any ancient
> text specifically foretelling their future.[17]

The Bible "is the only volume ever produced by man, or a group of men, in which is to be found a large body of proph-ecies relating to individual nations, to Israel, to all the peo-ples of the earth, to certain cities, and to the coming of One who was to be the Messiah."[18]

Many books have been written by some of the most com-petent scholars and well-educated individuals proving the validity of the Bible. Several are listed in the bibliography. In his book *Evidence That Demands a Verdict*, Josh McDowell, a graduate of Wheaton College and magna cum laude grad-uate of Talbot Theological Seminary, gives us an interesting comparison:

> There are now more than 5,300 known Greek
> manuscripts of the New Testament. Add over
> 10,000 Latin Vulgate and at least 9,300 other
> early versions (MSS) and we have more than
> 24,000 manuscript copies of portions of the New
> Testament in existence today. No other document
> of antiquity even begins to approach such num-
> bers and attestation. In comparison, the *Iliad* by
> Homer is second with only 643 manuscripts that
> still survive.[19]

DOES GOD USE DREAMS AND VISIONS?

I have had several dreams from the Lord in regard to the Bible. Even in very realistic dreams they are not analogous to an actual visit to hell.

Job said, "Then You scare me with dreams and terrify me with visions" (Job 7:14). The Book of Joel also mentions dreams and visions.[20] There are many examples where God gave a dream or a vision to someone for direction or warning. I believe my experience fits into the classification of a vision. In 2 Corinthians 12:1–2 Paul, in being "caught up to the third heaven," said, "I will come to visions...whether in the body...or whether out of the body I do not know."

At the time of his stoning and death, Stephen, looking up to heaven, saw "the Son of Man standing at the right hand of God" (Acts 7:56). He had not died yet when he saw the vision. Paul was on the road to Damascus when "suddenly a light shone around him from heaven. Then he fell to the ground, and heard a voice saying to him, 'Saul, Saul, why are you persecuting Me?'" (Acts 9:3–4).

Erwin W. Lutzer, who has graduate degrees from Dallas Theological Seminary, Loyola University, and Simon Greenleaf School of Law, said, "If Stephen saw our Lord before he died, and if Paul died and was caught up into paradise, it is just possible that other believers might also have such a vision....We should not expect such experiences, but they could happen."[21]

In Revelation 1:10 John said, "I was in the Spirit on the Lord's Day." Now, the Lord gave visions to these great men, and although my experience is not in any way to be compared to them, the Bible says that "God shows no partiality" (Acts 10:34). He will give a dream or a vision to anyone.

In Job 33:14–15 we read, "For God may speak…in a dream, in a vision of the night." In Numbers 24:4 Balaam was described as one who "hears the words of God, who sees the vision of the Almighty." Daniel 2:19 tells us that "the secret was revealed to Daniel in a *night vision*" (emphasis added). Obadiah 1 mentions, "The vision of Obadiah." Habakkuk 2:2 states, "Then the LORD answered me and said: 'Write the vision and make it plain.'"

Dr. Lester Sumrall had a vision from God in which he saw all of humanity walking down a very long, wide highway. He says:

> God lifted me up until I was looking down upon that uncountable multitude of humankind. He took me far down the highway until I saw the end of the road. It ended abruptly at a precipice towering above a bottomless inferno. When the tremendous unending procession of people came to the end of the highway, I could see them falling off into eternity. As they neared the pit and saw the fate that awaited them, I could see their desperate but vain struggle to push back against the unrelenting pressure of those to the rear. The great surging river of humanity swept them ever forward. God opened my ears to hear the screams of damned souls sinking into hell….I could see their faces distorted with terror. Their hands flailed wildly, clawing at the air.[22]

God told him that he would be responsible if he did not warn the people about their wicked ways.[23] That responsibility falls on all those who know Him. Dr. Lester Sumrall was a well-respected evangelist and pastor who established many churches, fed the poor on a large scale, preached the gospel for more than sixty-five years, and had many other accomplishments.

HAS ANYONE IN THE BIBLE EXPERIENCED HELL?

I wanted to know if there was any person in the Bible who had an experience in hell (*Sheol*).

Some theologians think that Jonah was in hell. Others think he was only at the "gates of hell." In Jonah 2:2 Jonah states: "I cried by reason of mine affliction unto the LORD, and he heard me; out of the belly of hell cried I, and thou heardest my voice" (KJV). Then he continues: "The earth with her bars was about me for ever: yet hast thou brought up my life from corruption, O LORD my God" (v. 6, KJV). The word *bars* in Greek is *bariyach*, which means "a relatively long, ridged piece of any solid material used for support or barrier." Whether he was *at* the gates or *inside* the gates is not the important issue. The fact is that he was there; that is what is relevant. This is not to place my experience on a level with Jonah, by any means. This is only to see what the Bible has to say about hell and his experience.

HAS ANYONE ELSE EXPERIENCED HELL?

There are others who were taken to hell or have had a glimpse of hell on their deathbed. Some of them have documented their experience through videos and books. These books are listed in the bibliography. I had no idea that these people existed. I had never heard of anyone having these experiences prior to my research. Their experiences are amazing. They seem to be reputable individuals—some doctors and other professionals. I am not endorsing their testimonies; neither am I disagreeing with them. They are most interesting. Below is one example.

In his book *Caught Up Into Paradise* Dr. Richard Eby mentions an experience where God gave him a two-minute vision of hell, in which he was placed in a pit. He was told that two minutes was all he could endure. He said, "Instantly I realized I was a dead sinner being taken to the lowest bowels of the earth. A sense of absolute terror gripped my being." In this pit small spiderlike demons were crawling all over him in total darkness and isolation. He said he knew he would never see another person and that he would never get out. Demons would taunt him, saying, "Damn God! Damn people!" He went on to say:

> And the smell! Horrid, nasty, stale, fetid, rotten and evil…mixed together and concentrated. Stinking, crawling demons mentally delighting in making me wretched. My terror mounted until I was ready to collapse into utter hopelessness, crushing despair, abysmal loneliness. I was an eternally lost soul by my own choosing…The clammy wet walls held me crushed for eternity without escape.[24]

As I have mentioned, there have been others who have experienced hell. I am not unique. However, any spiritual experience should be viewed in light of the Scriptures.

WHY WOULD GOD TAKE ME TO HELL?

I believe that the only reason God took me to hell was to draw attention to His Word on this subject. It is not that He needs my help or anybody else's. However, I believe time is getting short, and there are some unusual things God is doing in the earth today to help people awaken to the truth. He is imploring people to listen to His Word. This is not a condemning message but a warning message. God does not want anyone to go down the heavily traveled road that many are on.[25]

For the most part hell is not a popular subject in churches today. Many churches do not even believe or teach that hell is a literal burning place. The pastors in these churches do not want to offend their people by telling them there is a real hell to shun. Other people are offended by a message about hell and think Christians should keep their beliefs to themselves. I can understand that, and we should be very respectful of the beliefs of others. However, should we just be respectful and not give them warning? Try and look at it this way: You are sleeping in a hotel room, and it's very early in the morning. Someone starts yelling, "Fire! Fire!" You not only wouldn't mind that person waking you up, but also you would be extremely grateful for the warning if there was really a fire. The inconvenience would be welcomed in exchange for your life. Some people just don't realize there is a real fire to avoid.

One of the things the Lord said to me in that special time I shared with Him was, "Many of My people make excuses why they do not witness. They say, 'I did not feel led.' They fear man rather than fearing God." That statement pierced my heart. We all need to be led by the Holy Spirit, but so often we ignore the leading and make that excuse.

May we as Christians be sensitive to the Holy Spirit and watch for opportunities to share God's love and truth with others. Most of our witness is offered through our life example. Do we keep our word, are we quick to forgive, and do we show love and kindness even toward those who are mean to us? This speaks volumes to others. In addition, if we first care for others by helping or providing for their needs in a time of trouble, then we gain favor and have a right to speak into their lives. I like what one pastor said about witnessing. He said to first pray for people, then care for them, and then share with them.

We all have a part to do, and we are all called to be witnesses (Mark 16:15). We should never be judgmental or condescending with that witness but instead display a loving and caring attitude for others as we share His passion.

CHAPTER 7 NOTES

1. Chuck Missler, "Heaven and Hell—What Happens When You Die," Supplemental Notes to 66/40 Radio Broadcast with Chuck Missler, 2003, available as an audio CD, VHS videocassette, or DVD from Koinonia House, accessed January 16, 2017, http://www.khouse.org/articles/2003/491.

2. John Ankerberg and John Weldon, *Knowing the Truth About the Reliability of the Bible* (Eugene, OR: Harvest House, 1998), 24.

3. Ibid., 25.

4. Ibid., 26.

5. Robert Dick Wilson, *A Scientific Investigation of the Old Testament* (Chicago: Moody Bible Institute, 1959).

6. Ankerberg and Weldon, *Knowing the Truth About the Reliability of the Bible*, 22.

7. David Barton, *Original Intent* (Aledo, TX: WallBuilder Press, 2004), 168.

8. Arthur S. DeMoss, *The Rebirth of America* (West Palm Beach, FL: Arthur S. DeMoss Foundation, 1986), 37.

9. Barton, *Original Intent*, 168.

10. Ibid., 163.

11. Ibid., 164.

12. DeMoss, *The Rebirth of America*, 37.

13. Josh McDowell, *Evidence That Demands a Verdict* (Nashville: Nelson Reference, 1999), 15–17.

14. 2 Timothy 3:16.

15. McDowell, *Evidence That Demands a Verdict*, 20.

16. Ibid., 21.

17. Ibid., 22.

18. Ibid.

19. Ibid., 39.

20. Joel 2:28.

21. Lutzer, *One Minute After You Die*, 25.

22. Lester Sumrall, *Run With the Vision* (South Bend, IN: Sumrall Publishing, 1986), 32–33.

23. See Ezekiel 3:18; Acts 20:26–28.

24. Richard Eby, *Caught Up Into Paradise* (Grand Rapids: Fleming H. Revell Co., 1990), 229–30.

25. See Matthew 7:13.

CHAPTER 8

IMPORTANT FACTS ABOUT HELL

WHY WOULD GOD ALLOW ME TO EXPERIENCE PAIN IN HELL?

God blocked much of the pain I could have experienced in hell. However, He wanted me to be able to tell others that there will be literal pain felt in hell—that it is not simply metaphorical or allegorical. If that twenty-three minutes could motivate me enough to win more people to Christ, then that would serve His purpose. And it did motivate me to do just that!

God does not want us to suffer pain, and He does not inflict it upon us. The devil does that. God desires to bless us. Jesus said in John 10:10, "The thief does not come except to steal, and to kill, and to destroy. I have come that they may have life, and that they may have it more abundantly."

You might still ask, "Why would God allow you to feel any pain at all when He already paid the price?" First of all, I didn't "pay the price" for anyone's salvation by suffering the pain I did. That would be like saying, "Since Jesus suffered on the cross for us, then no Christian should ever bear any pain at any time for any reason."

In addition, I can answer your question with a question: Why did He allow the apostles to suffer the way they did? They were sawed in half, hung upside down on a cross, stoned, shipwrecked, thrown in dungeons, beaten, chained, and so forth. If God would allow even His best to suffer for the sake of the gospel, then how much more might I, who is not to be compared to any of those great men?

Besides, even though twenty-three minutes seemed like twenty-three weeks at the time, it was still only twenty-three minutes. What I experienced was minor in comparison with what the great men in the Bible experienced.

So there is suffering God allows for the sake of the preaching of the gospel. This suffering usually falls into the category of persecution. In 1 Corinthians 4:12 we read, "Being persecuted, we endure." Jesus reminded us, "If they persecuted Me, they will also persecute you" (John 15:20). Paul wrote, "Share with me in the sufferings for the gospel according to the power of God" (2 Tim. 1:8).

Many of the apostles suffered torturous deaths, stoning, beatings, and imprisonment because of their preaching of the gospel. In Acts 9:16 the Lord, speaking of Paul, said, "For I will show him how many things he must suffer for My name's sake." One example of Paul's suffering can be seen in Acts 16, where Paul and Silas were beaten and thrown into prison for preaching the gospel. If God would allow His own apostles to suffer, then how much more will He allow you and me to suffer! But He reminds us to remember this: "Let those who suffer according to the will of God commit their souls to Him in doing good" (1 Pet. 4:19).

Always keep in mind that our suffering must be in accordance with the will of God and not because of our own ignorance or disobedience to His Word, which can result in unnecessary suffering.

I believe the twenty-three minutes I spent in hell has caused me to accomplish more than I would have ever attempted to accomplish before the experience. The joy of seeing even one person come to Christ far outweighs any pain I experienced.

IS HELL A LITERAL BURNING PLACE?

Absolutely. The place is an inferno. I saw the pit—a mile across and consumed with fire. I saw the liquid fire that falls like rain. I felt the extreme heat, and I smelled the stench of burning things. I do not believe the Scripture references are merely symbolic or allegorical; I believe they speak of real fire. There are many important scriptures, and I urge you to read each one of them so that you can make your own informed decision. Appendix A is a comprehensive index of biblical references to hell. What God's Word says is far more important than the story of my visit to that place.

Both the Old and New Testaments provide evidence that hell is a literal burning place:

> But the wicked shall perish, and the enemies of the LORD shall be as the fat of lambs: they shall consume; into smoke shall they consume away.
>
> —PSALM 37:20, KJV

> For, behold, the day cometh, that shall burn as an oven; and all the proud, yea, and all that

do wickedly, shall be stubble: and the day that cometh shall burn them up, saith the LORD of hosts.

—MALACHI 4:1, KJV

...and will cast them into the furnace of fire.

—MATTHEW 13:42

I am tormented in this flame.

—LUKE 16:24

If a man abide not in me, he is cast forth as a branch, and is withered; and men gather them, and cast them into the fire, and they are burned.

—JOHN 15:6, KJV

...suffering the vengeance of eternal fire.

—JUDE 7

And he opened the bottomless pit; and there arose a smoke out of the pit...and the sun and the air were darkened by reason of the smoke of the pit. [The smoke literally darkened the sky. How could that happen unless there was an actual physical fire burning in the pit? It's not an allegorical or metaphorical fire, as many think or teach.]

—REVELATION 9:2, KJV

He shall be tormented with fire and brimstone.

—REVELATION 14:10

Thomas Vincent said:

Fire is the most affective and painful, therefore God has appointed fire to be for the punishment of the body.[1]

Charles Spurgeon said:

There is a real fire in hell, as truly as you now have a real body—a fire exactly like that which we have on earth in everything except this—that it will not consume, though it will torture you.[2]

There are many other Scripture verses on this point. (See Appendix A.)

WHAT IS HELL LIKE?

A lot can be said about what the experience of hell is like. You've already gained a sense of it through my description in the first part of this book of my experience of being thrust into that realm. Here I'd like to provide a summary of some key attributes of the place.

Dead but alive

It is difficult to explain how it is that you are dead in hell but still exist and feel pain. Death is separation from God, and God is the source of all life. Your soul lives on forever, yet it is disconnected from the source of all life (John 1:4).

It is, in a sense, like living in a negative—a piece of 35-millimeter film. It is not the true photo, with color and life. Rather, it is the reverse of the image, negative and lifeless. It is like being a shadow and not the real person. Daniel I. Block, in *Hell Under Fire*, described it as being like "living corpses" or "shadowy images."[3] According to *Harper's Bible Dictionary*, "The dead are referred to as 'shades,' pale reflections of the men and women they had once been (Isa. 14:10; Eccles. 9:10)."[4] *Matthew Henry's Commentary on the Whole Bible* says, "Their punishment will be no less than destruction…both as to body and soul. This destruction will be everlasting. They shall be *always dying, and yet never die.* Their misery will run parallel with the line of eternity."[5]

There is no way I can describe the horrendous feeling of being separated from God. It is the most empty, lonely, abandoned, and completely destitute feeling one could ever imagine.

Absence of good

Separation from God includes separation from all good. Many of us tend to think that the good things we experience, such as sunshine, fresh air, food, water, and beautiful scenery, are from Mother Nature. These things experienced are not from Mother Nature—but from Father God. James 1:17 states, "Every good gift and every perfect gift is from above, and comes down from the Father of lights." Hell, on the other hand, is a place "prepared" for the devil and his angels—a place where all of the attributes of God are completely withdrawn.

Psalm 33:5 states, "The earth is full of the goodness of the LORD." People get to enjoy God's goodness here in life. But if they deny Him, then after this life they will no longer have the privilege of enjoying His goodness.

There is no such thing as "good" without God. You cannot separate the two.

Not one drop

There is no water, ever—not even one drop—in hell. Deuteronomy 11:11 says that water is the "rain of heaven." It represents life (Rev. 21:6). But there is no life in hell (Rev. 6:8; 20:13–14), and therefore there is no water (Zech. 9:11).

My experience caused me to be much more appreciative of the things we take for granted in this life, such as a glass of water. My wife and I visited Niagara Falls once, where there is approximately 750,000 gallons per second coming over the falls. There is such an abundance of God's blessing here on the earth, and not one drop of this life-giving substance exists in hell.

The rich man depicted in hell in Luke 16 was desperate for just one drop of water, and so was I. If I were to give you a drop of water here on earth, you wouldn't value just one drop. But in hell you would. You would give anything for that drop, but you'll never get it.

The stench

A volcano spews burning rock, brimstone, and sulfur. Where do those things sound like they come from? I believe that through volcanos, God gives us a glimpse of hell. The spewing lava flow should be enough to scare anyone to at least think, "Hey, that might be what hell is like." I believe the lava flow and burning sulfur are a visual warning from God about hell below.

The odor of the sulfur in hell is similar to the toxic odor that emanates from a volcano. In Hawaii there are signs posted near the volcano that do not allow you to pass, as the fumes it produces are considered toxic.

I once received a call from a man who had a near-death experience and went to hell. He said he will never forget the sulfur odor in hell, so putrid and foul was it. After his experience of hell he was in Pearl Harbor, and he smelled that same odor. He wondered where it was coming from. A man told him that sometimes the trade winds carried the smell from the volcano on the big island, and they could smell it every so often. The man said it was the same foul smell he had encountered when he was in hell, and he would never forget it. Neither will I!

It is commonly known that sulfur has a pungent odor and is extremely foul. It is actually toxic. It is also known that *brimstone* is another word for sulfur. Brimstone, the Bible states, is found in hell. Job 18:15, 21 says, "Brimstone shall be scattered upon his habitation.... Surely such are the dwellings of the wicked" (KJV). Psalm 11:6 says, "Upon the wicked he shall rain snares, fire and brimstone, and an horrible tempest" (KJV). (See also Psalm 140:10; Isaiah 30:33; 34:9; Revelation 14:10; 20:10; 21:8.)

To add to the horrid smell of sulfur, Mark 9:25 states that Jesus rebuked a foul spirit. The odor was similar to that of an open sewer or rotting flesh and was extremely nauseating. It is the most disgusting stench imaginable.

A pastor we know who is also a police officer told us that on one occasion on patrol he came across a man who had been killed two weeks earlier. He was found in his apartment, and he was being eaten by maggots. The man said the stench was so disgusting that they vomited and later had to burn their clothes because the odor remained after washing. That is just from one body. Imagine thousands like that, along with sulfur, demons, and smoke!

Literal fire

The Bible is full of verses that describe hell as having a literal burning fire. I list many of those verses in this book. They speak for themselves. But let's see what Jesus and others have had to say about it.

Jesus used the word *Gehenna* to describe the future lake of fire eleven times. The people of His day knew what Gehenna represented. *Nelson's Illustrated Bible Dictionary* states:

> In the time of Jesus the Valley of Hinnom was used as the garbage dump of Jerusalem. Into it were thrown all the filth and garbage of the city, including the dead bodies of animals and executed criminals. To consume all this, fires burned constantly. Maggots worked in the filth. When the wind blew from that direction over the city, its awfulness was quite evident. At night, wild dogs howled as they fought over the garbage.
>
> Jesus used this awful scene as a symbol of hell. In effect he said, "Do you want to know what hell is like? Look at Gehenna."[6]

The rich man in Luke 16 says, "I am tormented in this flame" (v. 24, KJV).

Charles Spurgeon is quoted as saying:

> Do not begin telling me that that is metaphorical fire: who cares for that? If a man were to threaten to give me a metaphorical blow on the head, I should care very little about it: he would be welcome to give me as many as he pleased. And what say the wicked? "We do not care about metaphorical fires." But they are *real* sir—yes, as real as yourself. There is a real fire in hell, as truly as you now have a real body—a fire exactly like that which we have on the earth in everything except this—that it will not consume, though it will torture you.[7]

Jesus said in John 15:6, "If a man abide not in me, he is cast forth as a branch, and is withered; and men gather them, and cast them into the fire, and they are burned" (KJV). I believe that makes very clear the reality of fire in hell.

No mercy

The demons in hell have absolutely no mercy whatsoever. We have seen some of this lack of mercy in the terrorists who have sawed children's heads off. That lack of mercy comes from the demonic realm (Prov. 12:10; Matt. 23:33; John 8:44; Rev. 20:2–4). Psalm 103:17 states, "But the mercy of the LORD is...upon them that fear him." Those in hell do not fear the Lord, so they wouldn't derive that benefit.

God doesn't give us as believers what we deserve. He grants us mercy.

Confusion

Another thing that is difficult to describe is the utter confusion in hell. Hell is nothing but chaos and confusion. In life we like things in order. This is because we were created in God's image, who is a God of order (Exod. 40:4; Lev. 6:12; 2 Chron. 29:35; Ps. 119:133; Isa. 9:7; 1 Cor. 14:40; 16:1). These verses support the reality:

> A land of darkness...without any order.
>
> —JOB 10:22, KJV

> Their everlasting confusion shall never be forgotten.
>
> —JEREMIAH 20:11, KJV

> They shall go to confusion together that are makers of idols.
>
> —ISAIAH 45:16, KJV

No purpose

There is also no purpose of any kind in hell. All is over, lost, and gone. Ecclesiastes 9:10 says, "No work, nor device, nor knowledge, nor wisdom, in the grave [Sheol]" (KJV).

There is no reward for your accomplishments in hell. No fame, fortune, or status is recognized. In hell you have no identity. No one would know you even if you were famous. Ecclesiastes 6:4 says, "His name shall be covered with darkness" (KJV). Psalm 88:12 speaks of "the land of forgetfulness." In hell you are forgotten to all (Isa. 26:14).

Screams

I mentioned in my description of my experience the screams I heard in hell. I felt I couldn't bear for another minute how loud it was, with all the moaning, screaming, and gnashing of teeth.

Isaiah 32:18 says, "And my people shall dwell in a peaceable habitation...and in quiet resting places" (KJV). But in hell you are not His people—and so a quiet resting place will not be had by you. Isaiah 57:21 tells us, "There is no peace, saith my God, to the wicked" (KJV). There is no peace of mind and no peace of any kind. All there is, John Wesley said, is "one unvaried scene of horror upon horror! There is no music but that of groans and shrieks; of weeping, wailing, and gnashing of teeth; of curses and blasphemies against God."[8]

No rest

I mentioned in my description of hell how there would never be any enjoyment of sleep again, not even one moment of rest. The fear level is so high that it would not permit one to be at ease, even in the slightest. Besides, a person in severe pain cannot sleep.

Here are some related verses to describe this reality in hell:

> They have no rest day nor night.
>
> —REVELATION 14:10–11, KJV

> The wicked are like the troubled sea, when it cannot rest. [Sleep is a blessing from God.]
>
> —ISAIAH 57:20, KJV

> He giveth his beloved sleep. [But you are not His beloved there.]
>
> —PSALM 127:2, KJV

No strength

The Bible says, "The way of the LORD is strength for the upright" (Prov. 10:29)—but you are not His upright in hell. Isaiah 14:9–10 states, "Hell from beneath is moved for thee to meet thee at thy coming.... All they shall speak and say unto thee, Art thou also become weak as we?" (KJV). The word *weak* here is the same word used in Judges 16:7, where Samson became physically weak when his hair was cut off. According to *Strong's Exhaustive Concordance*, it means "weak, sick, afflicted."[9] Also, Psalm 88:4 says, "I am counted with those who go down to the pit; I am like a man who has no strength."

Most people in life enjoy strength, and in sports they train for their entire lives to get strength. We eat properly and sleep sufficiently to achieve the most strength and health possible. But the Bible says, "The joy of the LORD is [our] strength" (Neh. 8:10). God told Joshua, "Be strong" (Josh. 1:6). Caleb said he was strong like he was at forty, now being eighty-five (Josh. 14:11). David said, "The king shall have joy in Your strength, O LORD" (Ps. 21:1). It is God's strength we enjoy. Psalm 18:32 states, "It is God that girdeth me with strength" (KJV).

Movement in hell requires so much effort due to this lack of strength. We read in Acts 17:28, "For in him we live, and *move*, and have our being" (KJV, emphasis added). The word *move* here is the Greek word *kineo*, which means "to move, remove, to shake." It is also used in Matthew 23:4, where Jesus said, "For they bind heavy burdens...and lay them on men's shoulders; but they themselves will not move them with one of their fingers" (KJV). That is talking about physical movement.

You can see that even movement is given by God. Strength is a blessing from God. In hell it is the antithesis.

Can't breathe

In hell it is so very difficult to even capture one breath. It is far worse than a mountain climber being at too high of an altitude, where he cannot get adequate oxygen, or a person who has an asthma attack and can't breathe. This goes on forever.

Isaiah 42:5 says that God gives breath to people who dwell upon the earth—not to those *under* the earth. In the Bible the words *upon*, *beneath*, *below*, and *above* all are very specific, as is every word of the Bible. If you are in hell, then you are beneath the earth and therefore would not derive that benefit of the breath of God.

A spirit body

I mentioned in my description of the experience that I felt as though every bone in my body had been broken. I didn't say I had actual bones while I was there, but it felt like I did.

A spirit doesn't have bones (Luke 24:39), but the spirit

body (1 Cor. 15:44) feels the same as a physical body. Ezekiel 32:27 says, "But their iniquities will be on their bones." This is speaking with regard to those in the current hell, or Hades. Why mention bones if it's not something similar? And Psalm 141:7 says, "Our bones are scattered at the mouth of the grave [Sheol]."

The rich man, again, in Luke 16 had a mouth to speak and eyes to see, and he wanted a drop of water to cool his tongue. He felt the torment of the flame in a spirit body and was thirsty. Apparently a spirit body is similar in some ways to a physical body. You might think, "Why would a spirit need water?" Well, the rich man did! Spirit beings must still need water and possibly food. I felt hunger pains also in hell. However, you have no appetite there because you are extremely nauseated from the foul odors and don't want to eat.

In the wilderness the Israelites ate the manna from heaven. The Bible says it was "angels' food" (Ps. 78:25), but angels are spirit beings. Yet they eat manna, which could be consumed by humans. Did God convert the manna over for human consumption? Who knows! The point is, angels do eat, and they are spirit beings.

A spirit body is also eternal. Remember that the rich man was burning. This might cause you to ask, "Then why would he not be consumed?" It is because a spirit body is eternal. Remember the burning bush, which burned but "was not consumed" (Exod. 3:2).

Maggots

While I was in hell, I saw maggots by the millions crawling along the walls and on the ground. The Bible states over and over, "Where their worm dieth not, and the fire is not quenched" (Mark 9:44, KJV; see also Job 24:20; Isa. 66:24; Mark 9:46, 48). Notice it says *their* worm, not *the* worm. This means people have their own worms.

In *Vine's Complete Expository Dictionary* we read about "a worm which preys upon dead bodies."[10] Isaiah 14:11 states, "The maggot is spread under you, and worms cover you."

John MacArthur says in his teaching "The Furnace of Fire":

> When a body goes into the grave, into decay, worms descend into that body. And they begin to consume that body, and the worms will die when the food is gone. So once the body is consumed, the worms die. But in hell, the worms never die because the body, though it is continually being consumed, is never consumed....
>
> In other words, the Lord was saying the unrelieved torment of the body goes on and on.[11]

Just imagine maggots eating your flesh for eternity. That is a horrifying thought indeed!

On the edge

I was able, only for a few seconds in two different instances, to reflect on my life back here on the earth. Other than that I experienced the terror that fills your mind completely in hell, leaving no calm moments to ever escape in thought. My point is your mental escapes are ever so limited, as you are too occupied with fear and horror to ever have even a minute, only seconds, to reflect on your past.

You feel as if you will go completely insane—but the reality is you never do. You stay right on the edge. If you did actually go insane, it would be a form of escape, and there is no escape of any kind in hell, so insanity never quite occurs.

Remember the rich man in hell? He asked questions, seemed rational in his thinking, and understood why he was there. Those described in Ezekiel 32 also are aware of those around them, and they bear their shame. In order to bear shame, one would need to be rational. Otherwise they wouldn't realize the shame! So in hell you always stay right on the edge of rationality and irrationality, never quite tipping over into the escape of insanity.

Demons

There is one thing I want to point out about one of the demons I saw in the cell—the demon that seemed to look as if it had been in a battle. Chunks of its body were missing, and it appeared as if parts of its body were metal, as though metal had been used to replace some of the missing body parts. Now, there is actually a verse regarding metal on a demon, Revelation 9:9, which says, "And they had breastplates, as it were breastplates of iron" (KJV). John was describing what he saw when demons were coming out of the bottomless pit. I encourage you to read the rest of his description, as they were bizarre and terrifying creatures.

During the battle described in Revelation 12:4–8, Michael and his angels cast one-third of the fallen angels out of heaven. Perhaps this battle is where the fallen angels suffered loss and disfigurement.

There are other strange-looking demons in hell. Revelation 16:13 says, "And I saw three unclean spirits like frogs" (KJV). Read Ezekiel's vision of the four living creatures in Ezekiel 1 and in Ezekiel 10:9–14, 21–22. He is describing angels in heaven, but demons are fallen angels.

There are some strange-looking things in hell that are

difficult to describe, just like in heaven. I am simply reporting what I saw.

Keener senses

I noticed my senses were keener in hell. I could measure distances, could grasp eternity, and realized there was a whole world going on down there, with different levels of punishment.

In Zechariah 5:2, Zechariah tells of a vision he had: "And he said unto me, What seest thou? And I answered, I see a flying roll; the length thereof is twenty cubits, and the breadth thereof ten cubits" (KJV). Zechariah wasn't told the measurements of the roll, yet he knew them. How did he know them, and why is it recorded for us? This is only a hint of evidence about the way we know more in the spiritual realm. Again, going back to Luke 16, the rich man recognized Abraham and Lazarus. How did he know what Abraham looked like, especially from a great distance? He only knew because his senses were keener in the spirit realm.

Dr. Erwin Lutzer, a conservative and well-known scholar, said in his book *One Minute After You Die* that those in Sheol exist "with heightened perception and a better understanding."[12]

WHERE IS HELL LOCATED?

The current location for Sheol, or Hades, is down deep in the earth.

Forty-nine scriptures identify its location as under the earth. In essence this is the "first hell," so to speak. After Judgment Day, Death and Hell (Hades) will be delivered up and cast into "the lake of fire" (Rev. 20:12–15) and into outer darkness (Matt. 25:30). Jesus used the word *Gehenna* eleven times to describe the future hell, or lake of fire. So there are two separate locations for hell. No one is in the lake of fire at this time. Those who have already died who rejected Jesus Christ as their Lord and Savior are currently suffering in Hades, just as is the rich man mentioned by Jesus in Luke 16. Also, in Luke 16 the rich man was separated by a "great gulf fixed" (v. 26). That is a geographical description and not a state of mind.

In my experience I somehow knew that I was in the lower part of the earth, and I sensed it to be approximately thirty-seven hundred miles deep. It was as if my senses were keener or more aware than normal. I remember thinking, "Most people up on the earth's surface have no idea that there's a whole world going on down here below the surface. They don't know or wouldn't believe that so many are here." I remember falling to get there and ascending through the tunnel when I left.

The abyss is literally a shaft. Somewhere upon the surface of the Earth there is a shaft. The entrance to this shaft leads down into the heart of the Earth where Hades exists. Hades is often translated "Hell" in the Bible. Hell does exist. It is in the center of the earth.[13] —CHUCK SMITH

Pastor Chuck Smith, who wrote many books and was a very accomplished, well-respected senior pastor of one of the largest churches today for over forty years, stated in his book *What the World Is Coming To*, "Hell does exist. It is in the center of the earth."[14]

Smith also stated in that book:

When anyone from the Old Testament died, they went to Hades. That is why in the Old Testament Hades is referred to as the "grave" and "hell." It was the abiding place of everyone who died, but it was divided into two sections.... When Jesus died He descended into Hades and preached, according to Peter, to those souls in prison (1 Peter 3:19). According to Paul, when Jesus ascended He led these captives from their captivity (Ephesians 4:8). He emptied that portion of Hades where the faithful with Abraham had waited for God to fulfill His promises.[15]

Nelson's New Illustrated Bible Dictionary makes some interesting points about hell. In describing *Sheol* (hell), it says, "In Old Testament thought, the abode of the dead, *Sheol*, was regarded as an underground region."[16] It also gives a description of the word *pit*, saying it "is used in a theological way in both the Old Testament and New Testament. As a deep, underground place, *the Pit* became synonymous for *Sheol*, the abode of the dead."[17]

Jamieson, Fausset, and Brown's Commentary states, "'Paradise' and 'Abraham's Bosom,' the abode of good spirits in Old Testament times, are separated by a wide gulf from Hell or Hades."[18] It also says, "There has been placed a vast impassible abyss between the two states."[19]

Robert Jeffress said in his book *Outrageous Truth*:

Jesus firmly believed that hell is just as real a location as heaven. In John 14:2, Jesus promised His disciples, "I go to prepare a place for you." The Greek word for "place" is *topos*, which means "a geographical location." Heaven is not a state of mind, but it is the eternal destination for those who trust in Christ. In the same way, Jesus taught that hell was an actual destination rather than a state of mind. Read carefully how Jesus described the fate of the unrighteous: "These will go away into eternal punishment, but the righteous into eternal life" (Matthew 25:46).

My point is simply this: You can't have one group of people going to an actual location (heaven) and the other group of people going to a state of mind. Just as Jesus described heaven as a real place, He taught that hell is a real place.[20]

Some theologians state that it is in the center of the earth. Others don't know for certain. I believe Scripture is clear and speaks for itself. There are more than forty other verses on this point listed in Appendix A in addition to these verses that I am including here:

> And the earth opened her mouth, and swallowed them up....They...went down alive into the pit, and the earth closed upon them: and they perished from among the congregation.
>
> —Numbers 16:32–33, kjv

> "I saw a spirit ascending out of the earth....An old man is coming up."..."Why have you disturbed me by bringing me up?"
>
> —1 Samuel 28:13–15

> They are higher than heaven....Deeper than Sheol.
>
> —Job 11:8

But those who seek my life, to destroy it, shall go into the lower parts of the earth.

—Psalm 63:9

...in the lowest parts of the earth.

—Psalm 139:15

And the earth shall cast out the dead.

—Isaiah 26:19

...and even descended to Sheol.

—Isaiah 57:9

When I shall bring thee down with them that descend into the pit, with the people of old time, and shall set thee in the low parts of the earth, in places desolate of old, with them that go down to the pit.

—Ezekiel 26:20, kjv

For they are all delivered unto death, to the nether parts of the earth...with them that go down to the pit.

—Ezekiel 31:14, kjv

...when I cast it down to hell together with those who descended into the Pit.

—Ezekiel 31:16

Cast them down to the depths of the earth...with those who go down to the Pit.

—Ezekiel 32:18

Though they dig into hell...

—Amos 9:2

> For as Jonah was three days and three nights in the belly of the great fish, so will the Son of Man be three days and three nights in the heart of the earth. [Hades had two compartments, or two sides, separated by a great gulf fixed. On the one side was paradise; on the other side, torment.]
>
> —MATTHEW 12:40

> He [Jesus] also first descended into the lower parts of the earth.
>
> —EPHESIANS 4:9

Ezekiel 26:20 and Numbers 16:32–33 also make absolutely clear its location.

DO YOU HAVE A BODY IN HELL?

I certainly did. My body appeared to be the same as the one I have now, except there was no blood or water in it. Life exists in the blood, and water represents life. I was able to endure suffering that would have caused death to my current physical body immediately. Other than that it felt like a normal body, and all my faculties seemed to work. I could think, reason, and remember. My emotions were still there, and although my strength was almost nonexistent, my physical senses were acute—I could see, hear, touch, smell, and taste. What the Bible says about this is the important thing:

> Let us swallow them up alive like Sheol, and whole, like those who go down to the Pit.
>
> —PROVERBS 1:12

> Fear Him who is able to destroy both soul and body in hell.
>
> —MATTHEW 10:28

> ...that he may dip the tip of his finger in water
> and cool my tongue; for I am tormented in this
> flame.
>
> —LUKE 16:24

Luke 16:23–24 describes a man who had a tongue, eyes, and a mouth with which he spoke. He had some type of body. In addition, he recognized Abraham and Lazarus, so they must have had bodies to be seen and recognizable. Some experts say we will not have a body in heaven or hell until after Judgment Day. However, Jesus had a body after the Resurrection. Jesus said, "Handle Me and see, for a spirit does not have flesh and bones as you see I have" (Luke 24:39). When Jesus arose, Matthew 27:52–53 states that "the graves were opened; and many bodies of the saints who had fallen asleep were raised; and coming out of the graves after His resurrection, they went into the holy city and appeared to many." These saints had to have some type of physical body to be seen! The body we receive after the judgment will most likely be different, according to the Scriptures, than the body we would have after death at this time.

ARE THERE CHILDREN IN HELL?

The Bible implies that there are not. From the outlines of the people I saw, they seemed to be fully grown or adult in size. In addition, the screams I heard were not the screams of children; they were mature voices. I will say that I had an impression, an unexplainable internal feeling, that there were no children there. This was my experience. What the Word states is the only thing of concern:

[David] said…"I shall go to him, but he shall not return to me." [David wept over his child who died and stated that he would go to him.]

—2 SAMUEL 12:22–23

Unless you are converted and become as little children, you will by no means enter the kingdom of heaven.

—MATTHEW 18:3

Suffer [permit] little children, and forbid them not, to come unto me: for of such is the kingdom of heaven.

—MATTHEW 19:14, KJV

Whoever receives one of these little children in My name, receives Me.

—MARK 9:37

Let the little children come to Me, and do not forbid them; for of such is the kingdom of God. Assuredly I say to you, whoever does not receive the kingdom of God as a little child will by no means enter it.

—MARK 10:14–15

In his book *One Minute After You Die*, Erwin W. Lutzer states:

Children will not be in heaven because they are innocent. Paul taught clearly that children are born under condemnation of Adam's sin (Rom. 5:12)….If children are saved (and I believe they shall be) it can only be because God credits their sin to Christ; and because they are too young to believe, the requirement of personal faith is waived.[21]

The clear teaching of the Bible is that the souls of those children who die before they reach the age of understanding and responsibility are taken to the New Jerusalem with Christ to live joyfully with Him until the day of resurrection when they shall receive their own immortal body fit for eternity. I believe the Bible shows us that children will be in heaven.[22]

—GRANT JEFFREY

WHY IS HELL SO HORRIBLE?

Hell was not prepared for man but for the devil and his angels (Matt. 25:41). God never intended for man to go there. Even now He is preparing a place in heaven for those who make the right choice (John 14:2).

Why is hell so horrific? It's a place where God's attributes are not present. Many do not realize that all the good we enjoy is from God. Good doesn't exist apart from Him, in fact. James 1:17 states, "Every good gift and every perfect gift is from above, and comes down from the Father of lights." As Henry M. Morris and Martin E. Clark say in *The Bible Has the Answer*, "Essentially, hell is the place where all aspects of the presence of God will be completely withdrawn forever."[23]

The same word that is used in Matthew 25:41 for *prepared*, *hetoimazo*, where it says God prepared hell for the devil, is also used in John 14:2, where Jesus says, "I go *to prepare* a place for you" in heaven. Heaven is filled with all the attributes of His holiness and glory. But in God's preparation of hell He removed all of His attributes and goodness. Spiritual death means being separated from God and from all good. As a consequence this is the result:

- Hell is dark because "God is light" (1 John 1:5).

- Hell is only death because God is life (John 1:4).

- Hell is hatred because "God is love" (1 John 4:16).

- Hell has no mercy because the mercy of the Lord "is in the heavens" (Ps. 36:5).

- Hell is only weakness because the Lord is the giver of strength (Ps. 18:32).

- Hell is loud because, as God said, "My people will dwell in... quiet resting places" (Isa. 32:18).

- Hell has no water because water is "the rain of heaven" (Deut. 11:11).

- Hell has no peace because Christ is the "Prince of Peace" (Isa. 9:6).

The good we experience now is only because God allows us to enjoy it while we are here on the earth. Psalm 33:5 states, "The earth is full of the goodness of the LORD." However, if you want nothing to do with God, then a place has been prepared that has nothing to do with His goodness.

The fire in hell represents God's wrath. He pours out His wrath on sin in the form of fire (Ps. 11:6; 89:46; Jer. 4:4; Isa. 30:33; John 15:6; Heb. 10:27; Jude 7; Matt. 13:50; Rev. 14:10; 21:8). Robert Peterson wrote, "God is not present in hell in grace and blessing.... He is present in hell, not in blessing but in wrath."[24] However, God poured out His wrath on Jesus on the cross so we wouldn't have to take it. So it is our choice. We can either let Jesus take it for us, or we can take it by our rejection of Him as our Lord and Savior.

CHAPTER 8 NOTES

1. Vincent, *Fire and Brimstone*, 111–112.

2. Morgan and Peterson, eds., *Hell Under Fire*, 28.

3. Daniel I. Block, in *Hell Under Fire*, 58.

4. Paul Achtemeier, ed., *Harper's Bible Dictionary* (New York: Harper Collins, 1985), 365.

5. BibleStudyTools.com, *"Matthew Henry Commentary on the Whole Bible (Complete)*: 2 Thessalonians 1," emphasis added, accessed January 16, 2017, http://www.biblestudytools.com/commentaries/matthew-henry-complete/2-thessalonians/1.html.

6. Ronald F. Youngblood, ed., *Nelson's Illustrated Bible Dictionary*, new and enhanced ed. (Nashville: Thomas Nelson, 2014), 498.

7. Charles Spurgeon, as quoted in Morgan and Peterson, eds., *Hell Under Fire*, 28.

8. John Wesley, "Of Hell," sermon 73, as quoted by the Wesley Center Online, accessed January 16, 2017, http://wesley.nnu.edu/john-wesley/the-sermons-of-john-wesley-1872-edition/sermon-73-of-hell/.

9. "Strong's H2470—*chalah*," BlueLetterBible.org, accessed January 16, 2017, https://www.blueletterbible.org/lang/Lexicon/Lexicon.cfm?strongs=H2470&t=KJV.

10. *Vine's Expository Dictionary of New Testament Words*, s.v. "worm," accessed January 16, 2017, http://www.menfak .no/bibelprog/vines?word=%AFt0003395.

11. John MacArthur, "The Furnace of Fire," sermon preached May 9, 1982, transcript available at Grace to You, accessed January 16, 2017, http://www.gty.org/ resources/sermons/2304/the-furnace-of-fire.

12. Lutzer, *One Minute After You Die*, 39.

13. Chuck Smith, *What the World Is Coming To* (Costa Mesa, CA: Word for Today, 1993), 91.

14. Ibid., 91–93.

15. Ibid.

16. Youngblood, *Nelson's New Illustrated Bible Dictionary*, 1164.

17. Ibid., 96.

18. R. Jamieson, *Jamieson, Fausset, and Brown's Commentary on the Whole Bible* (Grand Rapids: Zondervan, 1999), 1477.

19. Ibid., 1013.

20. Robert Jeffress, *Outrageous Truth: Seven Absolutes You Can Still Believe* (Colorado Springs, CO: WaterBrook Press, 2008), 76.

21. Lutzer, *One Minute After You Die*, 73.

22. Grant R. Jeffrey, *Journey Into Eternity* (Minneapolis: WaterBrook Press, 2000), 219.

23. Henry M. Morris and Martin E. Clark, *The Bible Has the Answer*, rev. ed. (Green Forest, AR: Master Books, 1987), 311.

24. Peterson, *Hell on Trial*, 187, 200–201.

CHAPTER 9

UNDERSTANDING WHAT HAPPENS IN HELL

HOW COULD I "SEE" IN HELL?

Some people have asked me how I could see fire, pits, and desolate areas at all, since Scripture mentions "the blackness of darkness forever" (Jude 13; cf. 2 Pet. 2:17; Ps. 49:19). These verses refer to the time when death and hell are cast into the lake of fire and into outer darkness. (See Revelation 20:14; Matthew 25:30.) This will happen after Judgment Day.

Currently the hell we are talking about is *Sheol* or *Hades* and is not in outer darkness yet. But I believe, as Scripture states, that this also is a place of total blackness in the center of the earth. I could only see when I was near the large pit of raging flames. John Wesley said, "In the dreary regions of the dead...there is...no light but that of livid flames."[1]

Remember that in Luke 16:23 the rich man lifted up his eyes and *saw* Abraham and Lazarus "afar off," across a "great gulf fixed." How could he see them if it is total darkness?

ARE THERE PRISON CELLS AND BARS IN HELL?

I found myself in a prison cell, just as you would see on the earth. It had a barred, metal door and rough-hewn stone walls. I had an understanding that there were many such cells. But what I encountered in my experience can never compare to the truth of God's Word. There are several scriptures that speak of prison cells and bars.

In Proverbs 7:27 the Word indicates that hell is an inner room, a chamber that holds the sinner.

Prison cell

...descending to the chambers of death.

—PROVERBS 7:27

They will be gathered together, as prisoners are gathered in the pit, and will be shut up in the prison.

—ISAIAH 24:22

...who did not open the house of his prisoners?

—ISAIAH 14:17

He hath inclosed my ways with hewn stone. [Could be prophetic of hell.]

—LAMENTATIONS 3:9, KJV

...out of the low dungeon.

—LAMENTATIONS 3:55, KJV

Bars

They shall go down to the bars of the pit.

—JOB 17:16, KJV

Have the gates of death been revealed to you?

—JOB 38:17

You who lift me up from the gates of death...

—PSALM 9:13

...to the gates of death.

—PSALM 107:18

I shall go to the gates of Sheol.

—ISAIAH 38:10

The earth with its bars closed behind me forever; yet You have brought up my life from the pit.

—JONAH 2:6

And the gates of Hades shall not prevail against it.

—MATTHEW 16:18

...the keys of Hades and of Death.

—REVELATION 1:18

...having the key to the bottomless pit...

—REVELATION 20:1

Billy Graham said:

> The description of Satan's great power ends with the words, "who opened not the house of his prisoners" (Isa. 14:17). This undoubtedly refers to the prison house of Satan, Hades or the abode of the dead so clearly pictured in Luke 16:19–31.[2]

ARE THERE DEGREES OF PUNISHMENT IN HELL?

Yes, Scripture is very clear in regard to this point. During my experience I remember sensing that there were varying degrees of punishment. Some people were in worse situations than others—even though no area in that place would be even remotely tolerable. I remember thinking that it would also be far worse in the fire than in the cell. Again, examine the scriptures for yourself. I have also included some quotes from the theologians:

> This is the portion from God for a wicked man. [God is the One who appoints or assigns those who reject Jesus as their Lord and Savior to their rightful position in hell.]
>
> —JOB 20:29

> ...the sorrows God distributes in His anger...
>
> —JOB 21:17

> You have delivered my soul from the lowest depths of Sheol.
>
> —PSALM 86:13

> You have laid me in the lowest pit, in darkness, in the depths.
>
> —PSALM 88:6

> Just as the LORD of hosts determined to do to us, according to our ways and according to our deeds, so He has dealt with us.
>
> —ZECHARIAH 1:6

It will be more tolerable for the land of Sodom and Gomorrah in the day of judgment than for that city. [Verse infers a less tolerable situation in hell.]

—MATTHEW 10:15

He will reward each according to his works.

—MATTHEW 16:27

Therefore you will receive greater condemnation [inferring there is a lesser].

—MATTHEW 23:14

Ye make him twofold more the child of hell than yourselves.

—MATTHEW 23:15, KJV

…and will cut him in two and appoint him his portion with the hypocrites.

—MATTHEW 24:51

[One servant beaten with many stripes, another with few.]

—LUKE 12:42–48

…who "will render to each one according to his deeds."

—ROMANS 2:6

Anyone who has rejected Moses' law dies without mercy on the testimony of two or three witnesses. Of how much worse punishment, do you suppose, will he be thought worthy who has trampled the Son of God underfoot…?

—HEBREWS 10:28

And they were judged, each one according to his works.

—REVELATION 20:13

...shall have their part in the lake which burns with fire and brimstone.

—REVELATION 21:8

[Referring to Ezekiel 32:21] These heroic personages speak from the midst of Sheol, which may suggest that they are located in the heart of the netherworld, perhaps a more honorable assignment than "the remotest recesses of the pit."[3]

—DANIEL I. BLOCK

The holiness and justice of God demand that there will be different degrees of punishment that will accurately reflect the different evil deeds and motives of those who reject Christ's forgiveness.[4]

—GRANT R. JEFFREY

There will be degrees of separation, isolation and emptiness in hell.[5]

—DR. J. P. MORELAND

God's judgment will be intensely personal and individual. God will accurately weigh each person's individual responsibility. He will "give to each person according to what he has done."[6]

—SINCLAIR B. FERGUSON

CHAPTER 9 NOTES

1. John Wesley, "Of Hell."

2. Graham, *Angels: God's Secret Agents*, 105.

3. Morgan and Peterson, eds., *Hell Under Fire*, 50.

4. Jeffrey, *Journey Into Eternity*, 219.

5. Lee Strobel, *The Case for Faith* (Grand Rapids: Zondervan Publishing House, 2000), 180.

6. Morgan and Peterson, eds., *Hell Under Fire*, 223.

CHAPTER 10

DEALING WITH THE DEMONS OF HELL

ARE THERE DEMONS IN HELL?

The Bible states that there are demons in hell. I saw many by the pit, in the tunnel, and in the cell. They were all deformed and grotesque, and they ranged from small to enormous in size. The Bible says:

> Yet you [Satan] shall be brought down to Sheol, to the lowest depths of the Pit.
>
> —ISAIAH 14:15

> ...who did not open the house of his prisoners? [This is speaking of Satan in Sheol.]
>
> —ISAIAH 14:17

> Then He will also say to those on the left hand, "Depart from Me, you cursed, into the everlasting fire prepared for the devil and his angels."
>
> —MATTHEW 25:41

> For if God did not spare the angels who sinned, but cast them down to hell and delivered them

> into chains of darkness, to be reserved for
> judgment…
>
> —2 PETER 2:4

> And he opened the bottomless pit…out of
> the smoke locusts came…to torment them
> for five months….In those days men will seek
> death….The shape of the locusts was like horses
> prepared for battle…their teeth were like lions'
> teeth. And they had breastplates like…iron…the
> sound of their wings was like the sound of char-
> iots….They had tails like scorpions, and there
> were stings in their tails. Their power was to
> hurt men five months. And they had as king over
> them the angel of the bottomless pit.
>
> —REVELATION 9:2–11

On an audiocassette recording of John MacArthur he quotes a comment from the great saint John Bunyan, saying, "In hell thou shalt have none but a company of damned souls, with an innumerable company of devils, to keep company with thee."[1]

Erwin W. Lutzer points out, "If it is true that angels await those who have been made righteous by Christ, it is under-standable that demonic spirits would await those who enter eternity without God's forgiveness and acceptance."[2]

In Pastor Chuck Smith's book *What the World Is Coming To* he speaks about a book called *Through Forbidden Tibet* by Harrison Forman. Pastor Smith mentions the chapter titled "I Saw the King of Hell." He relates:

> He talks about an annual religious rite in Tibet
> where the religious men of the nation gather

and call forth various demons. At the conclusion of this weeklong ceremony, they call forth
the King of Hell. What he saw was uncanny. He
actually saw demons as they materialized, and
he describes them and their various forms. His
descriptions of the demons are much like those
in Revelation.[3]

Some have asked me, "Does the Bible support demons that
are twelve or thirteen feet tall?" On a tape series by Chuck
Missler he gives an explanation for the height of some of the
demons I saw in hell.[4] He speaks of the portion in the Book
of Genesis that describes "giants on the earth," which came
about as a result of the fallen angels that slept with women
and bore children who were called "mighty men" (Gen. 6:2–
4). He also refers to Jude, which talks about angels (fallen)
who didn't stay within their proper domain but who left their
abode and then gave themselves over to sexual immorality.[5]
"The remnant of the giants" is mentioned in Deuteronomy
3:11, where it specifically calls out a man whose iron bed was
approximately thirteen and a half feet long.

I'm sure you have heard the story of David and Goliath.
Goliath was over nine feet tall, and he wasn't alone. The
Bible says that Goliath had four other brothers, all giants,
and one even had twelve fingers and twelve toes (six per
hand and six per foot). (See 2 Samuel 21:20!) It is reasonable
to conclude that the unusually large size of men was a direct
result of contact with the fallen angels. The fallen angels
themselves were probably also very large. These evil angels
were cast down to hell, as mentioned in Jude 6–7 and 2 Peter
2:4. This is very well explained in Chuck Missler's tapes, who

in my opinion is one of the most exceptional scholars and teachers on the earth today.

DO DEMONS HAVE GREAT STRENGTH?

I believe the Bible indicates that demons have enormous strength. I can tell you from my experience that they exhibited great strength with me. They picked me up as if I weighed nothing. I had a sense that they were a thousand times stronger than a typical man. Please examine the verses for yourself:

> …His angels, who excel in strength…
>
> —PSALM 103:20

> …two demon-possessed men…exceedingly fierce, so that no one could pass that way.
>
> —MATTHEW 8:28

> There met Him…a man with an unclean spirit…and no one could bind him, not even with chains, because he had often been bound with shackles and chains. And the chains had been pulled apart by him, and the shackles broken in pieces, neither could anyone tame him.
>
> —MARK 5:2–4

> …angels, who are greater in power and might…
>
> —2 PETER 2:11

There may be some differences in fallen angels and demons, but that is another topic. Both demons and angels (not fallen angels but angels in general) are addressed in the above verses, both exhibiting great strength. Therefore it seems reasonable to conclude that it would be possible that demons in hell, or fallen angels, would have great strength also.

CAN DEMONS TORMENT PEOPLE ON EARTH?

Yes, they most definitely can and have done so, as you can see in Scripture. However, they cannot arbitrarily torment just anyone. They have to have a point of access, an entrance into an individual's life someplace. But that is another topic in itself. I have also cited one documented case for your review. The Bible gives evidence of the torment demons can cause to people on earth:

> So they cried aloud, and cut themselves, as was their custom, with knives and lances, until the blood gushed out on them.
>
> —1 KINGS 18:28

> So Satan went out from the presence of the LORD, and struck Job.
>
> —JOB 2:7

> There met him two demon-possessed men coming out of the tombs, exceedingly fierce.
>
> —MATTHEW 8:28

> ...cutting himself with stones [the demoniac].
>
> —MARK 5:5

> Then one of the crowd answered and said, "Teacher, I brought You my son, who has a mute spirit. And wherever it seizes him, it throws him down; he foams at the mouth, gnashes his teeth, and becomes rigid....And often he has thrown

him both into the fire and into the water to destroy him."

—MARK 9:17–18, 22

"A spirit seizes him...it convulses him...bruising him...." The demon threw him down and convulsed him.

—LUKE 9:39–42

Then he [an unclean spirit] goes and takes with him seven other spirits more wicked than himself, and they enter and dwell there; and the last state of that man is worse than the first.

—LUKE 11:26

And the Lord said, "Simon, Simon! Indeed, Satan has asked for you, that he may sift you as wheat."

—LUKE 22:31

...bringing sick people and those who were tormented by unclean spirits, and they were all healed.

—ACTS 5:16

A thorn in the flesh was given to me, a messenger of Satan to buffet me.

—2 CORINTHIANS 12:7

...quench all the fiery darts of the wicked one.

—EPHESIANS 6:16

Their power was to hurt men [referring to demonic creatures out of the bottomless pit].

—REVELATION 9:10

Demons cause pain and inflict people. Why? The Bible says, "The thief [Satan] does not come except to steal, and to kill, and to destroy" (John 10:10).

As I mentioned previously, in Lester Sumrall's book *Run With the Vision* he talks about a girl named Clarita Villanueva, a very famous case in the 1950s. This young girl was in a prison cell in Manila and was being bitten by devils right before the eyes of her captors. Sumrall writes:

> The Metropolitan radio and press of Manila, and the world press carried the sensational story. The *Manila Chronicle* stated on May 13, 1953: "Police medics probe case of girl bitten by Demons." The article then stated, "At least 25 competent persons, including Manila's Chief of Police, Col. Cesar Lucero, say that it is a very realistic example of a horrified woman being bitten to insanity by invisible persons. Villanueva writhed in pain, shouted and screamed in anguish...teeth marks, wet with saliva...all the time, all witnesses aver she was never able to bite herself. Other persons were excitedly saying, 'The girl is being choked by some unseen thing.' Another would say, 'Look, the marks of teeth appear.' Doctors, scientists, professors, legal experts, and even spiritualists had tried to help her, and all had failed."

> Your bodies shall be tormented in every part in the flames of hellfire…the pains of hellfire will be a thousand times more horrible and tormenting. Your bodies cannot now endure much pain without expiring…but hereafter God will strengthen your bodies to endure; they shall have…quicker sense and so much more capacity for pain….Your bodies shall roll and tumble in flames, and burn with horrible pain and yet never be consumed….I believe that the space of one quarter of an hour in hell will seem longer to the damned than a whole life of misery in this world.[6] —THOMAS VINCENT

Lester Sumrall "was granted an interview with Mayor Lacson of Manila to come to help her. The Mayor was visibly shaken by the hopelessness of the doctors before such strange phenomena." Lester was given permission to pray for her. He then cast the devils out, they left, and she recovered.[7]

CAN DEMONS TORMENT PEOPLE IN HELL?

The Bible says that demons will be in torment along with the people after Judgment Day, when death and hell are cast into the lake of fire and into outer darkness.[8] The Bible states in Revelation 20:10, "And the devil that deceived them was cast into the lake of fire and brimstone, where the beast and the false prophet are, and shall be tormented day and night for ever and ever" (KJV).

However, I believe Scripture indicates that currently in hell (*Sheol* or *Hades*), God does allow the demons to torment the lost souls. I have listed the verses that seem to infer this torment. This may not be absolutely conclusive in Scripture, and some theologians may disagree; however, I believe there are enough verses to consider this torment to be more than conjecture. What Scripture states is all that matters, not what I have to say. I am simply reporting the events that took place. I did experience this torment, and you can choose to believe me or not. Examine the verses, as Acts 17:11 states, and then decide for yourself.

The Bible tells us to search the Scriptures, and in doing so, there is a piecing together that often must take place in order to obtain an answer. In Isaiah 28:13 we read, "The word of the LORD was to them, 'Precept upon precept, precept upon precept, line upon line, line upon line, here a little, there a little." Proverbs 2:4 says to seek for wisdom, knowledge, and understanding as you would seek for "hidden treasures." Proverbs 25:2 states, "It is the glory of God to conceal a thing: but the honour of kings is to search out a matter" (KJV). So let's look at some Scripture verses.

Jesus said in Matthew 24:51, "...and will cut him in two and appoint him his portion with the hypocrites. There shall be weeping and gnashing of teeth." (See also Luke 12:46.) The Greek word *dichotomeo* means "to cut; to bisect; to cut asunder; 1) of the cruel method of punishment used by the Hebrews and others of cutting one in two; 2) cut by scourging, scourge severely."[9]

These two verses are talking about the severe punishment inflicted on those in hell. Some theologians say it does not literally mean *cut in pieces* or *cut in two*, but merely extreme torment or being cut off from God. That may or may not be. Either way, it defines the fact that hell is torment.

The next four verses describe what the Lord will do to those on the earth who rebel against His Word. However, is it possible that these verses serve as an inclusive punishment of hell also? I say this particularly because in the first three out of the four verses we will look at, the first line of the verses does directly talk about hell or Judgment Day:

> For a fire is kindled in mine anger and shall burn unto the lowest hell [Sheol]....They shall be burnt with hunger, and devoured with burning heat, and with bitter destruction: I will also send the teeth of beasts upon them, with poison of serpents of the dust.
>
> —DEUTERONOMY 32:22–24, KJV

The first verse is about hell; the second is about torment on the earth. However, "devoured with burning heat, and with bitter destruction" and "teeth of beasts" could be descriptive of hell also.

> He has set me in dark places, like the dead of long ago. He has hedged me in...made my chain heavy. Even when I cry and shout, He shuts out my prayer...blocked my ways with hewn stone...made my paths crooked...been to me a bear lying in wait, like a lion in ambush. He has turned aside my ways and torn me in pieces.
>
> —LAMENTATIONS 3:6–11

> For what good is the day of the LORD to you? It will be darkness, and not light. It will be as though a man fled from a lion, and a bear met him!...And a serpent bit him!
>
> —AMOS 5:18–19

Therefore they forgot Me...I will tear open their rib cage, and there I will devour them like a lion. The wild beast shall tear them.

—HOSEA 13:6–8

The adversaries of the LORD shall be broken in pieces.

—1 SAMUEL 2:10

The sorrows of Sheol surrounded me.

—2 SAMUEL 22:6

His soul draws near the Pit, and his life to the executioners.

—JOB 33:22

...you who forget God, lest I tear you in pieces.

—PSALM 50:22

...delivered him to the torturers.

—MATTHEW 18:34

...will cut him in two....shall be beaten with many stripes.

—LUKE 12:46–47

...nor complain, as some of them also complained, and were destroyed by the destroyer.

—1 CORINTHIANS 10:10

Opened the bottomless pit...came out... locusts...teeth of lions [description of demons out of the pit—they have the teeth of lions].

—REVELATION 9:2–8, KJV

Notice the repeated use of *lion* and *torn to pieces* and *tormentors* and *destroyers*. Who is doing the tearing in pieces, and who are the tormentors? Who is doing the beating "with many stripes" or the destroying?

Revelation 9:7–12 describes demons from the bottomless pit. In Pastor Chuck Smith's book *What the World Is Coming To* he states, "...had a king over them, which is the angel of the abyss [Satan] whose name in the Hebrew tongue is *Abaddon*, but in the Greek tongue has his name *Apollyon*....Both of these names mean 'destroyer.' Satan is a destroyer. He is the king over these demons."[10]

Dr. Grant R. Jeffrey, in his book *Journey Into Eternity*, draws an analogy and paints a picture for us with these words:

> Consider for a moment the companions who will share Hell with those who stubbornly resist God's mercy to the very end—Hitler, Stalin, plus every other murderer and torturer in history....Consider for one horrible moment what a normal citizen would experience if they were condemned to live in the worst penitentiary in North America, totally at the mercy of the wicked, perverted prisoners. Imagine that there were no guards or cell bars to protect you from the rage and cruelty of the merciless criminals who shared your jail....However, those who reject the salvation of Jesus Christ to the very end of their lives will face a situation far more horrible than the one suggested.[11]

Proverbs 15:29 says, "The LORD is far from the wicked." Hell is a place that is void of all good because all good things come from God. Everything we enjoy—such as fresh air, clean water, food, sunshine, freedom, health, pleasant temperatures, beautiful scenery, relationships, and so on—would not be possible if it were not for God. The Bible says, "Every good gift and every perfect gift is from above, and comes down from the Father" (James 1:17).

Dr. Charles Stanley, a senior pastor for thirty-five years of a large and well-respected church, has said, "People in hell will be separated from God and all that is good forever."[12]

I believe many of these verses that describe punishment of the rebellious on the earth are also revealing clues of what is entailed in hell's sufferings. However, if these verses are per-taining only to the suffering those without God will experi-ence on the earth, then how much more severe will it be in hell? I leave it for you to come to your own conclusions.

I hope this research has helped you become more aware of what the Bible has to say about this subject. Again, my expe-rience is only to draw attention to God's Word.

CHAPTER 10 NOTES

1. John MacArthur, "Hell—the Furnace of Fire," Tape #GC2304.

2. Lutzer, *One Minute After You Die*, 25.

3. Smith, *What the World Is Coming To*, 95.

4. Chuck Missler, "Return of the Nephilim."

5. Jude 6–7.

6. Vincent, *Fire and Brimstone*, 142–143, 149.

7. Sumrall, *Run With the Vision*, 119–129.

8. Matthew 5:20; Revelation 20:14.

9. *Strong's Exhaustive Concordance*, PC Study Bible V3.2F (www.biblesoft.com: BibleSoft, 1998), s.v. *dichotomeo*.

10. Smith, *What the World Is Coming To*, 97.

11. Jeffrey, *Journey Into Eternity*, 221.

12. Stanley, *Charles Stanley's Handbook for Christian Living*, 248.

CHAPTER 11

WRESTLING WITH THE BIG QUESTIONS

HOW CAN A CHRISTIAN SEE HELL?

The only way a Christian can see hell is in a vision or a dream. Mine was an out-of-body experience, which is classified as a vision. I didn't die. This also was not a near-death experience.

In Acts 2:17 the Bible says, "Your young men shall see visions, your old men shall dream dreams." God is giving people visions and dreams today because His Word says He will.

In Job 7:14 it says, "Then thou scarest me with dreams, and terrifiest me through visions" (KJV). In Isaiah 21:2 we see that Isaiah was given "a grievous vision" (KJV). And in Job 4:13–14 Eliphaz says, "The visions of the night...made all my bones shake." So God can give a person a terrifying, grievous, bone-shaking vision.

Paul said in 2 Corinthians 12:2, speaking of being caught up into heaven in a vision, "Whether in the body, I do not know, or whether out of the body I do not know." He didn't know what had fully transpired with his vision, whether it had happened in the body or out of it, but I was simply shown. The point is it is possible to travel in a vision in your spirit body (1 Cor. 15:44). We see this too in Ezekiel 8:3, where Ezekiel was picked up by his hair and carried from Babylon to Jerusalem in a vision.

Furthermore, in hell a person has a spiritual body. Matthew 10:28 says, "Fear Him who is able to destroy both soul and body in hell." In Luke 16 we see that the rich man had a mouth to speak and eyes to lift and wanted a drop of water to cool his tongue. He obviously had a spirit body that resembled a physical body. In Revelation, John, who was experiencing a vision, talked to an elder, ate, experienced his belly becoming bitter, and wept (Rev. 5:5; 10:10). He experienced the same things in his spirit body as a physical body would, all while he was in the Spirit (Rev. 4:2). And Daniel I. Block, in his contribution to the book *Hell Under Fire*, describes those in Sheol as carrying "a shadowy image of the whole person, complete with head and skeleton."[1]

Jonah is another person who experienced hell while alive. In Jonah 2:2 he says, "Out of the belly of Sheol I cried." A few verses later, in verse 6, he says, "The earth with its bars closed behind me forever." The *Tyndale Old Testament Commentary* states, "Jonah is on the verge of entering Sheol, and like a Palestinian city, Jonah views the underworld as having a gate, which was locked secure by bolts and bars."[2] In the *New International Commentary on the Old Testament* it says, "He had been in Sheol's belly."[3] Also, "The gates of hell prevailed against him, clanging shut with a terrible finality— or so it seemed."[4] Here is a believer who was either inside the gates or just outside the gates of Sheol.

This is not in any way to compare my experience to that of this great prophet or the others but merely to establish a scriptural basis for how this can occur. Again, I'm not trying to persuade anyone with my testimony but only to point people to the Word of God.

ISN'T GOD UNLOVING FOR SENDING PEOPLE TO HELL?

It is not God's decision if we go to hell. He gave that choice to us (Deut. 30:19). People choose to push God away and deny that Jesus is the only Way to eternal life. The Bible tells us how to stay out of hell (John 3:36; 14:6; Acts 4:12). We are also warned where we will go if we reject Jesus as our Lord and Savior and do not repent of our sins (Luke 13:3; Acts 17:30; Rev. 21:8). That is why Jesus said in Matthew 12:37, "For by thy words thou shalt be justified, and by thy words thou shalt be condemned" (KJV). If you have said you don't believe the Bible, your own words will condemn you. Don't forget too that the God whom people accuse of being unloving is the same One who suffered a horrific death on the cross to keep us out of hell!

All of us who are above the age of accountability are on the road to hell automatically. John 3:17–18 states that we are condemned already. This is because we are all born in sin (Ps. 51:1–5; 143:2; Rom. 3:10–12, 20, 23; 5:12). This is the reason Jesus came—to get us off that road we are on (John 12:47; Matt. 7:13–14; John 6:40).

Perry Stone says in *Secrets From Beyond the Grave*, on page 183, "All men are born under a death penalty, and if a person does not remove this sin penalty passed on through Adam, that person is separated from God."[5] The choice is ours.

SHOULDN'T A "GOOD" PERSON BE ALLOWED INTO HEAVEN?

We addressed this question already in chapter 6, but let's review it again through some new lenses.

Consider it this way: You wouldn't expect to get into another country by simply saying, "Let me in. I'm a good person." You need the proper credentials. You need a passport or visa for that country. In the same way, you need a relationship with Jesus Christ if you want to enter into His kingdom (Eph. 2:8–9; Titus 3:5; Rom. 3:10, 12, 20, 23, 28; Gal. 2:16; 2 Tim. 1:9).

Besides, God's opinion of good and ours are two different things. God's view of good is perfection (James 2:10; Ps. 19:7; Hab. 1:13). We would need to be perfect to gain entrance into His kingdom on that basis. If we lie once or steal once or lust once or even have one foolish thought, it is considered a sin. One sin would exclude us from heaven. That's a high standard.

So let me ask you: Do you meet those requirements? Are you perfect? Of course not—and none of us are. Thank God it is not based on our being good but on our having a relationship with Jesus Christ!

Another analogy will help us understand why "good" will not get us into heaven. Say you knock on the door of the most expensive home in the country and say to the residents, "Excuse me, but I'm moving in with you because I'm a good person." What do you think the owners of that home would say? No, right? Of course that's what they'd say. They don't know you. And their acceptance or refusal of you is not based on whether they are good or loving or whether you're a good person. It is dependent upon a relationship you do or do not have with them.

In the same way, we have to have a relationship with Jesus. God is not our Father if we reject Jesus. He offers to be our Father throughout our whole life, but we are the ones who reject Him. He is our Creator always, but He is not our Father until we invite Jesus Christ into our hearts as our Lord and Savior. Then He becomes our Father. At that point we have the privilege of living at His house (Rom. 3:28; Eph. 2:8–9; Titus 3:5; Gal. 3:26; John 1:12; 8:44; 17:9; Rom. 9:7–8; Eph. 5:5; Rev. 21:8; 1 Cor. 6:9; Prov. 24:9). So why would we expect to move into His house without knowing Him?

DOES OCCASIONAL SIN DESERVE ETERNAL PUNISHMENT?

This question starts with the wrong premise. It is not about time—whether a punishment should last forever—but about relationship. If it were based on time, that would be considered works. It would be like saying, "God, I paid off my sin by serving this time in hell." Our time is not valuable enough to pay for our sins. Only the shed blood of Jesus is valuable enough (Heb. 9:22). Ephesians 2:8–9 tells us we are saved by grace through faith, not by works. Therefore time has nothing to do with it.

In addition, God states that our sin *is* deserving of eternal punishment because sin is extremely offensive to God (Rom. 7:13), and this is because He is holy (Hab. 1:13). In the book *Hell Under Fire* Christopher W. Morgan states, "Sin is inherently against God, who is infinite in all His perfections. Thus, sin is an infinite evil and merits endless punishment."[6] Morgan goes on to give an analogy that shows us that the relationship with the offended party makes a difference. He writes, "If an angry teenage boy punched his mother, he would deserve more punishment than if he punched his older brother."[7] Similarly if we lied to our neighbor, it would not be as severe as if we lied in a courtroom to the judge. Robert A. Peterson quotes Thomas Aquinas in his book *Hell on Trial*, saying, "The higher the person against whom it is committed, the graver the sin."[8] Well, we have sinned against a perfect, holy, omnipotent, eternal God, and He is infinitely greater than any person and any position of man.

In addition, God is infinitely greater in not just position but also "being." If we killed a bug, it would be of no significance, even though it held life. But if we killed a dog or cat, that would be worse and deserving of some kind of punishment. Yet if we kill a human being, that would be far worse and deserving of a much greater punishment. And since God is infinitely greater in "being" than all of these, we have to comprehend the infinite magnitude of the One against whom we have sinned. Therefore our sin is deserving of an eternal punishment.

WHY CAN'T GOD LET SOMEONE OUT OF HELL AFTER A TIME?

This is a similar question to the last one. There are at least seven reasons why God cannot do this.

1. He cannot change or break His Word (Ps. 89:34; 119:89). God already stated exactly how to become "born again" in His Word (Gen. 15:6; Luke 13:3; John 3:3, 36; 14:6; Acts 17:30; Rom. 10:9–10; Eph. 2:8–9). Getting born again is the only way to stay out of hell, and time spent in hell would not merit receiving the new heart and spirit that is required.

2. We are saved by faith, not by sight. Once you are in hell, you see it exists, and it no longer requires faith to believe. The Bible says it is impossible to please God without faith (Heb. 11:6). Also, in Ephesians 2:8–9 we're told, "For by grace you have been saved through faith." (See also Galatians 2:16; Titus 3:5.)

3. *"Without shedding of blood there is no remission" (Heb. 9:22).* Our time spent in hell is not valuable enough to pay for sins. Only the shed blood of Jesus can acquire for us the forgiveness of our sins.

4. *Man is made in God's image, and since God is eternal, so is man (Gen. 1:26; Ps. 26:9; 34:22; 116:8; Isa. 38:17; Eccles. 12:7; Prov. 23:14; Job 33:28; 1 Kings 17:22; 1 Sam. 25:29).* Since we are eternal beings, God cannot annihilate us because that would violate His Word. He made us eternal beings because His intention was for us to live with Him forever in heaven. It was man's choice to disobey, thereby suffering the consequences.

5. *If man rejects Jesus as his Lord and Savior, there is no other place created for the soul to go.* All of creation was completed in Genesis 2:1. God cannot create another place for souls to go because He said at that time that it was finished. Remember, hell was not created but "prepared." In addition, we must realize that anything apart from God would be hell because all good comes from God (James 1:17).

6. *God cannot let an unrighteous person into heaven, as he would defile it, and God will not allow anything into heaven that defiles, profanes, or pollutes it (Rev. 21:27).* Time cannot give us a new heart and a new spirit, which is the requirement for entering heaven. Only trusting in His shed blood for our forgiveness of sins can do that (Ezek. 11:19; 18:31; 36:26; Jer. 24:7; Rom. 3:25; 5:8–9; 1 Cor. 15:3–4; 2 Cor. 5:21).

7. *God cannot allow someone into heaven just because He is merciful.* He is a holy God and a just God (Deut. 32:4; Ps. 89:14; 96:10; Prov. 11:1; Isa. 45:21; Acts 17:31). If God let someone off a punishment because He is merciful, it would violate His other attributes, such as justice and judgment. God is 100 percent just; therefore sin must always be punished (Rom. 6:23), and justice demands judgment. However, since God is also 100 percent love, He paid the price of suffering and death for us (Rom. 3:23–25; 5:9; 1 John 1:7; Eccles. 11:9; Prov. 20:9).

WILL THOSE WHO NEVER HEARD ABOUT JESUS GO TO HELL?

The Bible states that God is always completely fair and just (Deut. 32:4; Ps.7:9; 96:13; Eccles. 3:17). That means there is no one in hell unjustly. Only God knows who will go to heaven and who will not because He alone knows men's hearts. He is the Father of spirits (Heb. 12:9), and He commands the spirits of men (Num. 16:32; Job 34:14–15; Ps. 104:30; Eccles. 11:5; 12:7). However, the Scriptures are clear that God holds man accountable to search for Him and receive Him as Lord and Savior, mainly for just one reason: creation.

Romans 1 states that man is without excuse because of creation. It is obvious in creation there is design everywhere. Just look at one aspect of God's remarkable creation. Look at the human body, which is "fearfully and wonderfully made" (Ps. 139:14). Doctors spend a lifetime studying its intricate parts and only scratch the surface. Its design is obvious. This points to a designer, thereby leaving no excuse but to admit a Creator.

Man is held accountable because of the overwhelming evidence of design in creation. To say it all happened by accident or to attribute it to some dumb idol is to abandon all reason. It is not as if man doesn't know. He knows, but he chooses to push God away anyway. Romans 1:25 states, "Instead of believing what they knew was the truth about God, they deliberately chose to believe lies" (TLB).

If the man in the remote jungle cries out and says, "God, I know You exist. Please reveal Yourself to me," God will make Himself known to that man in some way (1 Chron. 28:9; Acts 17:27; Rom. 10:13; 1 Tim. 2:4; 2 Pet. 3:9).

Here are just four ways God has made us accountable:

1. He has given us a conscience to know there is a God and to know right from wrong (John 8:9; Rom. 2:15). He also has placed eternity in man's heart (Eccles. 3:11).

2. He gave us the Bible, which is the truth. The truth is placed in writing in a book that has been scrutinized by thousands. There has not been one discrepancy found that couldn't be cleared up by the Scripture itself or by good scholarship, according to the scholars. It is the most sound, trustworthy, and accurate book ever written. And in the Bible the directions to heaven are clearly defined (John 3:16, 36; 8:24; 14:6; Acts 4:12; 1 Cor. 15:3–4; 1 Tim. 1:15; 1 John 5:12).

3. He sends missionaries around the world. People hear the truth through such faithful people. In addition, TV, radio, the Internet, CDs, and more are used to get the message out (Ps. 2:8; Prov. 9:1–3; Rom. 10:14–18).

4. He gives us dreams and visions to keep back our souls from the pit (Job 33:15–18). God will warn people in dreams and visions.

These next verses show us that all men everywhere are accountable to repent and to acknowledge Jesus Christ as Lord and Savior:

The wicked shall be turned into hell, and *all* the nations that forget God.

—Psalm 9:17, emphasis added

Unless you repent you will *all* likewise perish. [Jesus speaking.]

—Luke 13:3, emphasis added

"…shall be beaten with many stripes. But he who *did not know*, yet committed things deserving of stripes, shall be beaten with few." [Not knowing is no excuse.]

—Luke 12:47–48, emphasis added

"He who believes in the Son has everlasting life; and he who does not believe the Son shall not see life, but the wrath of God abides on him."

—John 3:36

"That *all* should honor the Son just as they honor the Father." [Jesus speaking.]

—John 5:23, emphasis added

"For if you do not believe that I am He, you will die in your sins." [Jesus speaking.]

—John 8:24

God…now commands *all* men everywhere to repent.

—Acts 17:30, emphasis added

For *all* have sinned and fall short of the glory of God.

—Romans 3:23, emphasis added

> Wherefore, as by one man sin entered into the world, and death by sin; and so death passed upon all men, for that *all* have sinned.
>
> —ROMANS 5:12, KJV, EMPHASIS ADDED

> And the *whole* world lieth in wickedness.
>
> —I JOHN 5:19, KJV, EMPHASIS ADDED

> *Every* spirit that confesseth not that Jesus Christ is come in the flesh is not of God.
>
> —I JOHN 4:3, KJV, EMPHASIS ADDED

You can see by these verses that all men everywhere are accountable to repent. I don't think we can be dogmatic about it one way or the other, as God is the judge and knows man's heart. However, in saying that, it is my opinion the Scripture is clear, that all men everywhere must repent and confess Jesus as their Lord and Savior, or they will not be allowed to enter heaven.

IS HELL ETERNAL, OR ARE THOSE IN HELL SIMPLY ANNIHILATED?

The Bible is explicitly clear that hell is eternal. Jesus said in Matthew 25:46, "These will go away into everlasting punishment, but the righteous into eternal life." The word for *eternal* is *aionios*. It is the same word used with regard to heaven and hell. Since those in heaven are eternal, so are those in hell. Similar verses are found in John 5:29, Mark 16:16, Daniel 12:2, and Acts 24:15.

Revelation 14:10–11 states, "He shall be tormented with fire and brimstone in the presence of the holy angels, and in the presence of the Lamb: and the smoke of their torment ascendeth up for ever and ever: and they have no rest day nor night" (KJV). They are in His presence, so they must exist. Also, you have to exist to have "no rest day nor night."

Again, in Luke 16, the rich man was in the current hell (Sheol or Hades) and was in torment in the flame. Some say this story was only a parable. However, according to most commentaries and scholars, it was not. No parable Jesus told ever included a specific name in it. This one has three names. Also, Jesus said in verse 25, "But Abraham said…" Notice Jesus is quoting Abraham saying something. If this were a parable, then it would not have been Abraham saying anything. Jesus would have been lying because Abraham would not have been speaking. That is proof it was a true story.

But even if it was a parable (and it wasn't), then tell me what it means. The man said he was in torment in the flames. He also said a person would need to repent in order to avoid hell. He was concerned for his brothers coming there. Why would he be concerned about that if all those in hell are going to be annihilated? Jesus would have really missed the point if He knew no one goes to hell or all are eventually let out! The so-called parable would not have drawn that conclusion.

Revelation 20:13 states that "death and hell [Hades, which is not the future lake of fire] delivered up the dead which were *in them*: and they were judged every man according to their works" (KJV, emphasis added). How can hell deliver up those "which were in them" if they do not exist? And why would they be judged if they were simply annihilated?

There are many verses on degrees of punishment (Matt. 10:15; 16:27; 23:14–15; Luke 12:47; Heb. 10:28–29), and we looked at these in a previous chapter. Why have varying degrees of punishment if all are going to be annihilated? In addition, what did Jesus save us from if all of us are going to be annihilated?

In Matthew 25:46 Jesus used the phrase "everlasting punishment." Even the word *punishment* denotes an existence. The word for *punishment* is the Greek word *kolasis*, which means "torment." How can a person be tormented if he does not exist?

Again, God made us in His image, so we are eternal beings (Gen. 1:26; 35:18; Ps. 26:9; Isa. 38:17; Eccles. 12:7; Prov. 23:14; Ps. 116:8; 34:22; Job 33:28; 1 Kings 17:22; 1 Sam. 25:29). We will exist forever. Death does not mean "cease to exist." It means "separation from God." One still exists in one place or the other.

Again, the Scriptures bear this out:

> There will be wailing and gnashing of teeth. [Must exist to gnash!]
>
> —MATTHEW 13:42

> It were better for him that a millstone were hanged about his neck, and that he were drowned in the depth of the sea. [Indicating something coming that is worse than death.]
>
> —MATTHEW 18:6, KJV

> ...to be cast into everlasting fire. [Why have everlasting fire?]
>
> —MATTHEW 18:8, KJV

> ...to go into hell, into the fire that never shall be quenched.
>
> —MARK 9:43, KJV

Be not afraid of them that kill the body, and after that have no more that they can do. But I will forewarn you whom ye shall fear: Fear him, which after he hath killed hath power to cast into hell. [Why warn of something that is worse than death if there is nothing?]

—LUKE 12:4–5, KJV

...suffering the vengeance of eternal fire.

—JUDE 7, KJV

He shall not depart out of darkness. [That statement presupposes their existence.]

—JOB 15:30, KJV

Brimstone shall be scattered upon his habitation.... Surely such are the dwellings of the wicked. [One would have to exist to *dwell* in a place.]

—JOB 18:15, 21, KJV

They shall never see light. [Must still exist to never see light.]

—PSALM 49:19, KJV

Hell from beneath is moved for thee to meet thee at thy coming.... They shall speak and say unto thee, Art thou also become weak as we? [Must still exist to be able to speak.]

—ISAIAH 14:9–10, KJV

Who among us shall dwell with everlasting burnings? [How is one burned "everlasting" if one does not exist?]

—ISAIAH 33:14, KJV

For their worm shall not die, neither shall their fire be quenched; and they shall be an abhorring unto all flesh. [Must still exist to be seen by others.]

—Isaiah 66:24, kjv

The strong among the mighty shall speak to him out of the midst of hell. [Must still exist to speak.]

—Ezekiel 32:21, kjv

Her company is round about her.... They borne their shame.... Their iniquities shall be upon their bones. [Must exist to bear shame.]

—Ezekiel 32:23, 24, 27, kjv

...some to everlasting life, and some to shame and everlasting contempt. [One would have to exist to experience everlasting shame and contempt.]

—Daniel 12:2, kjv

If hell is not eternal, then why did Jesus say about Judas in Matthew 26:24, "But woe unto that man by whom the Son of man is betrayed! It had been good for that man if he had not been born" (kjv). If there is nothing following death, then why make that statement? (Also see 2 Thessalonians 1:9; Luke 3:17; Jude 13; 2 Peter 2:17; Isaiah 38:17–18; 45:16; Malachi 4:1; Jeremiah 20:11; Proverbs 9:18.)

WHY DO SOME PEOPLE WHO HAVE NEAR-DEATH EXPERIENCES SEE A BRIGHT LIGHT?

There may be at least two reasons why.

First, Ecclesiastes 3:20–21 states, "And all turn to dust again. Who knoweth the spirit of man that goeth upward...?" (KJV). Ecclesiastes 12:7 says, "And the spirit will return to God who gave it." Since our spirit returns to God, it stands to reason that a person dying would first approach God. Since "God is light" (1 John 1:5), it may be that he sees His presence or an angel. Many near-death experiences report this light, even if the person is not a believer in the Lord.

There have been others who also approached this light, but as they became closer, they were directed to another path, a dark path, with loud screams, heat, and demons. They were terrified. Perhaps as they reach the Lord, He or an angel sends them in the direction of hell if they are not believers. Those who have not traveled that far in the tunnel now think it's all peaceful and full of light.

The second possible reason is that the Bible states that Satan can appear as an "angel of light" (2 Cor. 11:14). Could they have seen Satan and not realized they were being deceived? These are just possibilities.

Some report having seen their dead relatives before they ever reached heaven. Could they have seen "familiar spirits," as the Bible calls them in Leviticus 19:31 and 20:6? A familiar spirit is one that is familiar with your family members and can appear to resemble them, for the false hope that all is well. In reference to demons, *Vine's Expository Dictionary of New Testament Words* states:

> They disseminate errors among men, and seek
> to seduce believers, 1 Tim. 4:1. As seducing

spirits they deceive men into the supposition that through mediums (those who have "familiar spirits," Lev. 20:6, 27, e.g.) they can converse with deceased human beings. Hence the destructive deception of spiritism, forbidden in Scripture, Lev. 19:31; Deut. 18:11; Isa. 8:19.[9]

Familiar spirits can gain entrance into the lives of those who have experimented with occult practices, such as fortune-telling, tarot cards, palm reading, sorcery, kabbalah, astral projection, witchcraft, and the like (Deut. 18:10–12; Acts 19:18–19; 2 Kings 21:6; 2 Chron. 33:6), or occult objects, such as Ouija boards, hallucinogenic drugs, religious artifacts, and the like. (If you have ever participated in these activities, ask God for forgiveness and to release you from their effects.)

There have been many accounts reported in books about people who have had near-death experiences and seen this bright light. Dr. Maurice Rawlings, MD, a specialist in cardiovascular diseases who was the personal physician at the Pentagon and who has studied many cases of near-death experiences, in one of his books, *Beyond Death's Door*, states, "The light appeared in the 'good' experiences and seemed to represent acceptance for all people. There was a sense of universal forgiveness, according to some."[10] He goes on to say, "Some theologians remind us that Satan does not always appear evil but is...capable of the most clever deception. He can transform himself into an angel of light to convince the unsaved they are already saved or to neutralize the necessity of the Christian gospel."[11] Additionally he says:

> In each account, however, the person is returned to his body before any decision is reached or any disposition is rendered. This initial encounter could conceivably represent a sorting ground. It could also represent a deceivingly pleasant situation to imply security and sanctuary and to prevent a desire or need for changed lives.[12]

Also, in his book *To Hell and Back* he says, "Why are most of the reports beautiful? If Satan should appear as Lucifer to be the angel of light, the victim might feel secure and comfortable in the seduction of this angelic fate."[13] Satan knows that if he can show up at a person's death and appear as this peaceful angelic personage (2 Cor. 11:14; Gal. 1:8), then that individual will believe there is no judgment or hell. He is the master deceiver, and Revelation 12:9 says, "...Satan, who deceives the whole world." He must be masterful at deception to fool the whole world! However, he cannot appear to everyone who has a near-death experience, as he is not omnipresent; God is.

The area in which Satan wants to deceive people the most is in regard to their eternity. He knows he will forever be stationed in the lake of fire, and he wants to take as many people with him as possible. He hates God and therefore wants to hurt God's highest creation: you and me!

CHAPTER 11 NOTES

1. Daniel I. Block, in *Hell Under Fire*, 58.

2. T. Desmond Alexander, "Jonah: An Introduction and Commentary," in *Obadiah, Jonah, Micah*, ed. D. J. Wiseman, Tyndale Old Testament Commentaries, vol. 26 (Downers Grove, IL: IVP Academic, 2009), 114–16.

3. Leslie C. Allen, "The Book of Jonah," in *The Books of Joel, Obadiah, Jonah, and Micah*, The New International Commentary on the Old Testament Series (Grand Rapids: Wm. B. Eerdmans, 1976), 216.

4. Ibid., 217.

5. Perry Stone, *Secrets From Beyond the Grave: The Amazing Mysteries of Eternity, Paradise, and the Land of Lost Souls* (Lake Mary, FL: Charisma House, 2010), 183.

6. Morgan, *Hell Under Fire*, 210.

7. Ibid.

8. Peterson, *Hell on Trial*, 109.

9. *Vine's Expository Dictionary of New Testament Words*, s.v. "demon," accessed January 16, 2017, http://www.menfak.no/bibelprog/vines.pl?word=demon.

10. Maurice Rawlings, MD, *Beyond Death's Door: The Life After Life Bestseller* (New York: Bantam, 1979), 98.

11. Ibid., 100.

12. Ibid., 70.

13. Maurice Rawlings, MD, *To Hell and Back: Life After Death—Startling New Evidence* (Nashville: Thomas Nelson, 1993), 99–100.

SHOUTS OF VICTORY

So MUCH GOODNESS has happened as a result of that November night many years ago. God gave me an experience that shook the foundation of my world, and I could not help but go out and share what I'd seen with others. God knew that it would take such a foundation-shaking experience to get this reserved conservative in gear!

Here, at the end of this tenth-anniversary edition of *23 Minutes in Hell*, I'd like to leave you with a victory shout. Below I've shared a small sampling of the triumphant work of God that has been shared with us over the years as a result of this message. My prayer is that these testimonials boost your faith and help set you further along the path of bringing the love of God into this world through you.

> Thank you, Mr. Wiese, for signing one of your books for a prisoner. We played your video for about ninety inmates, and more than twenty of them got saved.
>
> —B. G.

> I was just drawn back after some time to reread my copy of your book. I am now thinking of

buying it in multiple copies and spreading it in strategic locations. One great asset of the book is that it has the "can't put it down" intrigue, fear, horror, and raw insight into what many want to deny. I love the on-the-spot biblical references for all to investigate and ponder. Just want to say that next to God's blessed Word, the greatest book of all time by far is *23 Minutes in Hell*, and it is going to be my strongest tool to spread around my corner of the world.

—J. D.

Your book has really touched my heart. I must admit, before I opened this book I was agnostic. Your book has made me realize that I need God in my life. I am a thirteen-year-old girl, and I want to be saved and not end up in hell. I can't thank you enough for opening my ears to hear that God will never leave my side. I am blessed I found this book.

—T.

I have heard your testimony through the years and saw you the other night on TBN. You did an amazing job, and your memory of Scripture is impeccable. Thank you very much for your courage to stand up for Jesus Christ.

—M. M.

I picked up a copy of your book. What touched me most was the attitude of Jesus toward those who are being lost. Now I know with certainty that Jesus wants all men to be saved. After I read your book, I went to church the next Sunday. I

went forward and gave my entire self to fulfilling
the call of God on my life.

—Anonymous

I am fifteen years old, and I just read your book
23 Minutes in Hell. When I got to high school,
things got harder. I've been drawing away from
God. I didn't really involve Him in my life.
When I read the book (in one day), it immediately changed me. I felt [as if] I just wanted to be
with God. I immediately prayed with God after
I read it. I'm so happy to know that God does
care for me and loves me. I want to thank you so
much for that book. It saved my life! I am sure
that book is changing so many lives and [that]
so many more people are going to be with God
because of what you saw and are sharing.

—J.

This book got me off the fence and into *not* being
afraid to share my faith! I have bought several
of these books and given them away! I absolutely
believe that God allowed you, Bill, to visit hell so
that you could tell others how horrible and terrifying it is. I have *never* heard such a descriptive
interpretation of this awful place!

—J. M. C.

I was saved because of this man's testimony! I'm so
grateful that he was obedient to tell of his experience. I will not be going to hell now because I
received a good scare and wake-up call and asked
God to spare me from this horrid place! I was
one of those people [who] never read the Bible,

but I did buy this book for some odd reason, and God used it to save me! I believe God sent this man to hell to come back and tell about it for stubborn people like myself who wouldn't find it in the Bible that I was not reading. I got saved after I read *23 Minutes in Hell*, so I'm extremely grateful!

—M. P.

Your video has really changed my life. A bit less than two years ago I was considering suicide. I had been living in the world for a long time, and I was very ill and tired. I simply could not see any way out. I was looking on YouTube for ways to kill myself when someone I know said not to do it but to look at Bill Wiese's video *23 Minutes in Hell* instead. I watched it, and I got scared. I knew if I had died, I would go to hell, so I called a friend who was a Christian and asked her if I could come with her to church. I did, and I gave my life to Jesus shortly after that. My life has completely changed. Now I live for Jesus, and He is my everything. I am an artist and a rapper, and now I use that for God's glory. Thank you so much for your video and testimony. God used it to reach me. God bless you.

—T. B.

You definitely want to get this book. Thank you for sharing! *23 Minutes in Hell*, although it took me a couple of years to get up the nerve to read, has forever changed me! It has given me a passion to witness like I never had before. It has given me the ability to love people despite their actions and lifestyles that I wouldn't have had without this very vivid description of hell and what anyone will be going through without Jesus. May God continue to use you and bless you!

—C. T.

Bill and Annette, I thank God for you both. Thank you for being obedient to the Lord in writing about your experience. It has caused me to rededicate and recommit my life to Jesus. My entire family has rededicated our lives to Jesus. Today I received a shipment of your book to give to family, friends, and strangers. Thank you again for your humbleness and obedience. Because of it so many souls are spared from the flames of hell, including [mine and my family's]. I am eternally grateful to my Lord and Savior for a second chance.

—L.

I would just like to say thank you for this book. It was truly life-changing. I have been a Christian my whole life but have never really done a whole lot to help save others from the terrors of hell. I'm eighteen and still in high school. I have so many friends that need to hear this message. I will deliver it to them and do my part for the kingdom of God. Thank you for opening my eyes and possibly saving more people.

—M. M.

I have a ministry that goes into a detention center in Illinois. Today was our movie day, where we showed the DVD *23 Minutes in Hell*. We are only allowed fifteen men for the movie. The results...unbelievable! A third of them raised their hands to be saved, and the remaining two-thirds rededicated their lives to Christ. These are men who regularly come to a weekly Bible study, and many of the men are federal prisoners who are doing hard time and will go to one of the many federal prisons throughout the country.

—K. M.

I wanted to let you know what a blessing your book was to my mom. My mom was a member of Scientology for over thirty-five years. I became a Christian at fifty years old and sent her a copy of your book. At the age of ninety-four she became a Christian. We know God was the reason; your book sure helped! Thank you.

—J. B.

I am a science major in a top-school program. I strongly repelled the notion of God previously. I considered myself a smart girl and a good person, but it was hard to believe the Bible and God. Then I got sick and started praying with a par-tial faith that Jesus would show me something to help me believe in Him. Somehow I came across your testimony on YouTube. You totally convinced me. I know why God picked you, Bill. You are not the fame-chasing type who tried to get popular by lying about things. Just seeing how sincere, serious, shy, and reserved you are and how you left your career made me believe in you and the loving/weeping arms of Jesus. I have gone from "Religious people are weak and have a lack of science knowledge" to "I love Jesus, and I am willing to give my life to Him. He is so full of wisdom. How dare I compare myself to Him?" You are the living and current proof that I need to strengthen my faith, and God used you to save me. You are my frequency to God's kingdom. I believe in your testimony, hell, and God.

—C. Z.

Your book changed my life, and I am so grateful. I am compelled to lead people to Christ.

—N. L.

I read your book, and it changed my life. Thank you, Bill, for your book and the work that you do for God.

—J. P.

I read your book. I tell everyone they need to read it. It will help you realize that we need to be spreading the gospel so they will not end up in that horrible place for eternity. Thank you for writing your story.

—N. B.

I'm a pastor, and *23 Minutes in Hell* rocked me! I am so thankful to God that I will not spend eternity in hell. But I am thankful to Bill Wiese for sharing his experience. I wish everyone in the world could hear this message. If they could, I know it would save them. Thank you, man of God, for telling your story.

—D. B.

Four years ago I listened to this, and the fear of the Lord fell on me, and I gave my heart to the Lord!

—S. B.

Love this man! A wonderful, wonderful man and testimony. Powerful and true man of God. Saw him in person. My husband accepted the Lord under his testimony in Tulare about three years ago. Read his book too. Great testimony every person should read.

—E. G.

God has trusted you with a ministry that is so needful in these times of so much evil and fear of the unknown! I can't imagine what you were feeling when you were sent to that awful place! But God chose you, I believe, because He knew you would not fail to tell everyone about such a place! And you and your precious wife, Annette, have not failed to do exactly what He has called you to do! Thank you for your passion and concern for a lost and dying world! God bless you both!

—B. A.

I just want to say *thank you* for changing my life forever. Before I read your testimony (and saw the video), I did not completely believe in hell. I did think, rather foolishly, that heaven was the default place we all go to when we die, as many preach it today (even so-called Christian books). Boy, was I wrong! For the first few days I was completely shocked. I have to admit, even my very soul was shaken by this revelation. Only then did I start to fully understand why Jesus died for us and what the good news is all about! For the first time in my life, at age thirty-eight, I understand Christ's message and the high price He paid for us. And for that I will be forever grateful. I accepted Christ once again (but now it is truly 100 percent) as my Lord and Savior, and I am ready to pass on the message to other people. I started right away with my kids. My life will be different forever because of you. God bless you for having the courage to share this message!

—M. S.

I gave my life to the Lord Jesus Christ through your video on YouTube. I wouldn't know anything about truth if it were not for your testimony. I love the Lord Jesus Christ, and He has washed me in His blood.

—N. B.

Bill's *23 Minutes in Hell* experience is the best witnessing and salvation message on the planet. If you have a loved one who is not saved, give them this book. People die every minute without repentance of their sins and without Christ as their Lord and Savior. If you don't know where you will go if you die tonight, you need to read Bill's book. Heaven is for real, and so is hell.

—P. C.

God bless you, brother, for stepping out and sharing this divine revelation the Lord gave you. As a pastor I recommend your story to everyone

I can so they will know there is a hell, and, more importantly, there is a way to heaven.

—M. S.

I wanted to thank you. After watching *23 Minutes in Hell* and rewatching it, I got baptized two weeks ago. I study the Bible and am deeply into the Lord Jesus Christ more than ever. You and your beautiful wife led me because of your testimony. I finally found a church, and I am so tearfully grateful because of your signpost that led me to the right way. I watched every YouTube video of *23 Minutes in Hell,* and it changed my life forever. Thank you so much, and praise God!

—C. W.

SCRIPTURE INDEX

APPOINTED OR ASSIGNED

1 Kings 20:42	Thus saith the LORD...a man whom I appointed to utter destruction... (KJV).
Job 21:17	The sorrows God distributes in His anger...
Proverbs 31:8	...all such as are appointed to destruction (KJV).
Matthew 24:51	...and will cut him in two and appoint him his portion with the hypocrites.
Luke 12:46	...will cut him in two and appoint him his portion with the unbelievers.
Revelation 21:8	All liars shall have their part in the lake which burns with fire and brimstone.

BODY IN HELL

Proverbs 1:12	Let us swallow them alive like Sheol, and whole like those who go down to the Pit.
Matthew 5:29	...whole body to be cast into hell.
Matthew 10:28	Fear Him who is able to destroy both soul and body in hell.

DARKNESS

1 Samuel 2:9	But the wicked shall be silent in darkness.
Job 10:21–22	Before I go to the place from which I shall not return, to the land of darkness and the shadow of death, a land as dark as darkness itself, as the shadow of death, without any order, where even the light is like darkness.
Job 18:18	He is driven from light into darkness, and chased out of the world.
Job 33:28	He will redeem his soul from going down to the Pit, and his life shall see the light.
Job 33:30	...to bring back his soul from the Pit, that he may be enlightened with the light of life.

Psalm 49:19	They shall never see light.
Psalm 88:6	You have laid me in the lowest pit, in darkness, in the depths.
Proverbs 20:20	Whoever curses his father or his mother, his lamp will be put out in deep darkness.
Nahum 1:8	And darkness will pursue His enemies.
Matthew 8:12	...will be cast out into outer darkness.
Matthew 25:30	Cast the unprofitable servant into the outer darkness.
2 Peter 2:4	...cast them down to hell and delivered them into chains of darkness...
2 Peter 2:17	...for whom is reserved the blackness of darkness forever.
Jude 13	...for whom is reserved the blackness of darkness forever.
Revelation 16:10	...and his [the beast] kingdom became full of darkness.

DEGREES OF PUNISHMENT

Proverbs 9:18	Her guests are in the depths of hell.

Zechariah 1:6   Just as the LORD of hosts determined to do to us, according to our ways and according to our deeds, so He has dealt with us.

Hebrews 10:28–29   Anyone who has rejected Moses' law dies without mercy on the testimony of two or three witnesses. Of how much worse punishment, do you suppose, will he be thought worthy who has trampled the Son of God underfoot?

DESTRUCTION

Job 21:30   The wicked are reserved for the day of doom.

Job 31:3   Is it not destruction for the wicked, and disaster for the workers of iniquity?

Job 31:23   For destruction from God is a terror to me.

Psalm 9:17   The wicked shall be turned into hell, and all the nations that forget God.

Psalm 16:10   For You will not leave my soul in Sheol, nor will You allow Your Holy One to see corruption.

Psalm 32:10   Many sorrows shall be to the wicked.

Matthew 23:33   How can ye escape the damnation of hell? (KJV)

Matthew 24:51   There shall be weeping and gnashing of teeth.

Matthew 25:30   There will be weeping and gnashing of teeth.

Luke 13:3   Unless you repent you will all likewise perish.

Luke 16:23   And being in torments in Hades, he lifted up his eyes and saw Abraham afar off.

Romans 3:16   Destruction and misery are in their ways.

2 Thessalonians 1:9   These shall be punished with everlasting destruction from the presence of the Lord and from the glory of His power.

2 Peter 2:9   ...to reserve the unjust under punishment for the day of judgment.

ETERNAL SEPARATION

Proverbs 15:29   The LORD is far from the wicked.

2 Thessalonians 1:9   These shall be punished with everlasting destruction from the presence of the Lord.

FEAR

Job 18:14	And they parade him before the king of terrors.
Job 31:23	For destruction from God is a terror to me.
Psalm 55:4	The terrors of death have fallen upon me.
Psalm 73:18–19	You cast them down to destruction. Oh, how they are brought to desolation, as in a moment! They are utterly consumed with terrors.
Proverbs 10:24	The fear of the wicked will come upon him.
Hebrews 10:31	It is a fearful thing to fall into the hands of the living God.

FIRE/BURNING

Deuteronomy 32:22	For a fire is kindled in My anger, and shall burn to the lowest hell.
Job 18:15	Brimstone is scattered on his dwelling.
Job 31:12	For that would be a fire that consumes to destruction.

Psalm 11:6	Upon the wicked He will rain coals; fire and brimstone and a burning wind shall be the portion of their cup.
Psalm 37:20	The enemies of the Lord shall be as the fat of lambs: they shall consume; into smoke shall they consume away (KJV).
Psalm 140:10	Let burning coals fall upon them; let them be cast into the fire; into deep pits, that they rise not up again.
Isaiah 66:24	And their fire is not quenched.
Matthew 5:22	Whoever says, "You fool!" shall be in danger of hell fire.
Matthew 13:30	Let both grow together until the harvest, and at the time of harvest I will say to the reapers, "First gather together the tares and bind them in bundles to burn them, but gather the wheat into my barn."
Matthew 18:8	... to be cast into the everlasting fire.
Matthew 18:9	... to be cast into hell fire.
Matthew 25:41	... into the everlasting fire.
Mark 9:43	... rather than having two hands, to go to hell, into the fire that shall never be quenched.

Mark 9:44	...where their worm does not die and the fire is not quenched.
Mark 9:45	...rather than having two feet, to be cast into hell, into the fire that shall never be quenched.
Mark 9:46	...where their worm does not die and the fire is not quenched.
Mark 9:47	...rather than having two eyes, to be cast into hell fire.
Mark 9:48	...where their worm does not die and the fire is not quenched.
Luke 3:9	Every tree which does not bear good fruit is cut down and thrown into the fire.
Luke 3:17	But the chaff He will burn with unquenchable fire.
James 3:6	And it is set on fire by hell.
Revelation 9:2	And smoke arose out of the pit like the smoke of a great furnace.
Revelation 20:10	...was cast into the lake of fire and brimstone...and they will be tormented day and night forever and ever.

HELL

Psalm 55:15	Let them go down alive into hell.
Psalm 88:3	My life draweth near to the grave (KJV).
Psalm 139:8	If I make my bed in hell, behold, You are there.
Proverbs 5:5	Her steps lay hold of hell.
Proverbs 9:18	Her guests are in the depths of hell.
Proverbs 27:20	Hell and Destruction are never full.
Isaiah 5:14	Sheol [hell] has enlarged itself.
Habakkuk 2:5	He enlarges his desire as hell.
Matthew 16:18	The gates of hell shall not prevail against it (KJV).
Matthew 23:33	How can you escape the condemnation of hell?
Luke 12:5	But I will show you whom you should fear: Fear Him who, after He has killed, has power to cast into hell, yes, I say to you, fear Him!
2 Peter 2:4	Cast them down to hell.
Revelation 20:14	Death and Hades were cast into the lake of fire.

HELL DESOLATE (NO LIFE OF ANY KIND)

Isaiah 59:10   We are as dead men in desolate places.

Ezekiel 26:20   I will make you dwell in the lowest part of the earth, in places desolate from antiquity, with those who go down to the Pit.

HUMILIATION/SHAME (ENDURED IN HELL)

Isaiah 5:14–15   Therefore Sheol has enlarged itself and opened its mouth beyond measure.... People shall be brought down, each man shall be humbled.

Isaiah 5:15   People shall be brought down... and the eyes of the lofty shall be humbled.

Isaiah 57:9   ... and even descended to Sheol.

Ezekiel 32:24   Now they bear their shame with those who go down to the Pit.

Revelation 16:15   Blessed is he who watches, and keeps his garments, lest he walk naked and they see his shame.

LIFE SHORT

Psalm 39:5	You have made my days as handbreadths.
Psalm 102:3	For my days are consumed like smoke.
Psalm 103:15–16	As for man, his days are like grass...for the wind passes over it, and it is gone.
James 4:14	For what is your life? It is even a vapor that appears for a little time and then vanishes away.

LOCATION

Deuteronomy 32:22	For a fire is kindled in My anger, and shall burn to the lowest hell.
Job 11:8	They are higher than heaven...deeper than Sheol.
Job 33:24	Deliver him from going down to the Pit.
Job 33:28	He will redeem his soul from going down to the Pit, and his life shall see the light.
Psalm 9:15	The nations have sunk down in the pit.

Isaiah 14:9	Hell from beneath is moved for thee to meet thee at thy coming (KJV).
Isaiah 14:19	But you are cast out of your grave like an abominable branch...who go down to the stones of the pit, like a corpse trodden underfoot.
Isaiah 38:18	For Sheol cannot thank You, death cannot praise You; those who go down to the pit cannot hope for Your truth.
Isaiah 44:23	Sing, O heavens, for the LORD has done it! Shout, you lower parts of the earth. [Paradise indicated to be in the lower part of the earth before the ascension of Jesus.]
Isaiah 57:9	...and even descended to Sheol.
Lamentations 3:55	...from the lowest pit.
Ezekiel 26:20	Then I will bring you down with those who descend into the Pit, to the people of old, and I will make you dwell in the lowest part of the earth, in places desolate from antiquity, with those who go down to the Pit.
Ezekiel 28:8	They shall throw you down into the Pit.

Ezekiel 32:30	...who have gone down with the slain...and bear their shame with those who go down to the Pit.
Amos 9:2	Though they dig into hell...
Matthew 11:23	...will be brought down to Hades.
Matthew 12:40	...so will the Son of Man be three days and three nights in the heart of the earth.
2 Peter 2:4	...but cast them down to hell and delivered them into chains of darkness...
Revelation 9:1	...to the bottomless pit.
Revelation 20:1, 3; 9:1–2; 17:8	...the bottomless pit.

NO HOPE

Job 8:13	And the hope of the hypocrite shall perish.
Proverbs 11:7	And the hope of the unjust perishes.
Ecclesiastes 9:4	But for him who is joined to all the living there is hope.
Isaiah 38:18	Those who go down to the pit cannot hope for Your truth.

NO MERCY

NO PEACE

NO PURPOSE

Psalm 6:5	For in death there is no remembrance of You.
Psalm 88:5	...whom You remember no more.
Psalm 88:12	...in the land of forgetfulness...
Proverbs 10:28	But the expectation of the wicked will perish.
Ecclesiastes 6:4	And his name shall be covered with darkness (KJV).
Ecclesiastes 9:10	...for there is no work or device or knowledge or wisdom in the grave.

NO REST (FROM TORMENT; ALSO NO PHYSICAL REST OR SLEEP)

Isaiah 57:20	...when it cannot rest.
Revelation 14:11	And the smoke of their torment ascends forever and ever; and they have no rest day or night.

ODORS/STENCH

Mark 9:25	He [Jesus] rebuked the foul spirit (KJV).
Revelation 18:2	...a prison for every foul spirit.

PIT

Job 33:24	Deliver him from going down to the Pit.
Job 33:28	He will redeem his soul from going to the Pit.
Job 33:30	...to bring back his soul from the Pit, that he may be enlightened with the light of life.
Job 33:18	He keeps back his soul from the Pit.
Psalm 30:3	...that I should not go down to the pit.
Psalm 30:9	...when I go down to the pit...
Psalm 40:2	He also brought me up out of a horrible pit.
Psalm 55:23	But You, O God, shall bring them down to the pit of destruction.
Psalm 143:7	Do not hide Your face from me, lest I be like those who go down into the pit.
Isaiah 38:17	But You have lovingly delivered my soul from the pit of corruption.

Isaiah 38:18	For Sheol cannot thank You, death cannot praise You; those who go down to the pit cannot hope for Your truth.
Ezekiel 32:23	Her graves are set in the recesses of the Pit.
Ezekiel 32:25	Yet they bear their shame with those who go down to the Pit.
Ezekiel 32:29	...and with those who go down to the Pit.
Ezekiel 32:30	...and bear their shame with those who go down to the Pit.
Revelation 9:1	To him was given the key to the bottomless pit.
Revelation 9:2	And he opened the bottomless pit, and smoke arose out of the pit like the smoke of a great furnace.
Revelation 11:7	...the beast that ascends out of the bottomless pit...
Revelation 17:8	The beast that you saw was, and is not, and will ascend out of the bottomless pit.
Revelation 20:3	And he cast him into the bottomless pit.

PRISON

Proverbs 7:27   ...is the way to hell, descending to the chambers of death.

Isaiah 24:22   They will be gathered together, as prisoners are gathered in the pit, and will be shut up in the prison.

PROFANITY

Ezekiel 22:26   ...so that I am profaned among them [vulgar and blasphemous language].

Ezekiel 28:14–16   You were the anointed cherub who covers...therefore I cast you as a profane thing [Satan profane].

RIGHTEOUS JUDGE

Deuteronomy 16:18   And they [judges] shall judge the people with just judgment.

Deuteronomy 16:20   You shall follow what is altogether just.

Deuteronomy 32:4   ...for all His ways are justice, a God of truth and without injustice; righteous and upright is He.

Psalm 7:9   ...for the righteous God tests the hearts and minds.

Psalm 96:10	He [God] shall judge the peoples righteously.
Psalm 96:13	He shall judge the world with righteousness, and the peoples with His truth.
Proverbs 11:1	...a just weight is His delight.
Proverbs 17:26	To punish the righteous is not good.
Ecclesiastes 3:17	God shall judge the righteous and the wicked.
Isaiah 45:21	...a just God and a Savior.
Zechariah 8:16	Give judgment in your gates for truth, justice, and peace.
Acts 17:31	He will judge the world in righteousness.

THIRST

Zechariah 9:11	I will set your prisoners free from the waterless pit.

TORMENT ON EARTH FROM SATAN OR DEMONS

1 Kings 18:28	...and cut themselves...until the blood gushed out on them.

TORMENT IN HELL

Psalm 74:20	...for the dark places of the earth are full of the haunts of cruelty.
Psalm 116:3	And the pangs of Sheol laid hold of me; I found trouble and sorrow.
Amos 5:18–19	It will be darkness, and not light...leaned his head on the wall, and a serpent bit him.
Matthew 24:51	...and will cut him in two....There shall be weeping and gnashing of teeth.
Luke 12:47–48	...shall be beaten with many stripes...shall be beaten with few.

WORMS

Job 21:26	They lie down alike in the dust, and worms cover them.
Job 24:20	The worm should feed sweetly on him.
Isaiah 14:11	The maggot is spread under you, and worms cover you.
Isaiah 66:24	...for their worm does not die.
Mark 9:44	...where their worm does not die.
Mark 9:46	...where their worm does not die.

Mark 9:48	...where their worm does not die.

WRATH

Exodus 15:7	You sent forth Your wrath.
Job 21:30	The wicked are reserved for the day of doom; they shall be brought out on the day of wrath.
Job 31:23	Destruction from God is a terror to me.
Psalm 73:27	For indeed, those who are far from You shall perish; You have destroyed all those who desert You for harlotry.
Psalm 90:7–11	We have been consumed by Your anger, and by Your wrath we are terrified....Who knows the power of Your anger?
Proverbs 11:23	The expectation of the wicked is wrath.
Isaiah 66:15	...to render His anger with fury.
Jeremiah 4:4	...lest My fury come forth like fire, and burn so that no one can quench it.
Jeremiah 25:37	...of the fierce anger of the LORD.
Lamentations 4:11	The LORD has fulfilled His fury, He has poured out His fierce anger.

COMMENTS ON HELL FROM THE "HALL OF FAME"

MANY PEOPLE HAVE studied God's Word and other resources to understand the subject of hell. Often their study is based on personal experiences of their own or the experiences of others. Often it is carefully researched from the annals of theology and historical fact. In my research of the subject after my experience in hell, some of these "Hall of Famers" have provided me with tremendous insight and support of what I experienced for myself in hell.

In Part II, Research After the Return: Questions and Answers About Hell, and in Appendix A, the scripture index, I have provided you with the scriptural information and knowledge about hell I gathered during my own research. Without a doubt, what God's Word has to say about hell—or about any other subject—is the authoritative guide for your life and mine.

As you have been reading my book, you have been able to read many "Hall of Fame" quotes about the topic of hell. These were inserted as additional evidence of the realities of what I saw during my experience. However, you may also find it enlightening to read the additional quotes from "Hall of Famers" included in this appendix.

THE ASSEMBLIES OF GOD

> There will be a final judgment in which the wicked dead will be raised and judged according to their works. Whoever is not found written in the Book of Life, together with the devil and his angels, the beast and the false prophet, will be consigned to everlasting punishment in the lake which burneth with fire and brimstone, which is the second death. (Matthew 25:46; Mark 9:43; Revelation 19:20; 20:11–15; 21:8.)[1]

CORAL RIDGE PRESBYTERIAN CHURCH

> At death, man's soul leaves his body and goes either to Heaven or to Hell...those who are impenitent and unsaved shall be cast into outer darkness forever. Sadly, we declare that we believe in the conscious eternal punishment on the unsaved.[2]

EDWARD DONNELLY

> The doctrine of Hell should lead us to appreciate more than we do the love and merits of the Lord Jesus Christ....From how much have we been spared?[3]
>
> The doctrine of hell should make believers supremely contented, grateful to God in every circumstance of life.[4]

JONATHAN EDWARDS

Eternal punishment is not eternal annihilation. Surely they will not be raised to life at the last day only to be annihilated.[5]

MILLARD J. ERICKSON

Nothing in Scripture indicates that there will be opportunity for belief after a preliminary period of punishment.[6]

JOHN MACARTHUR

No one in scripture spoke more of judgment than Jesus. He spoke of sins that could not be forgiven, of danger of losing one's soul forever, of spending eternity in the torments of Hell, of existing forever in outer darkness, where there shall be weeping and gnashing of teeth.[7]

CHUCK MISSLER

Sinners are warned to "flee from the wrath to come" (Matt 23:33; Luke 3:7). At the last judgment every person will be resurrected and judged individually, and there will be an accounting of every detail of each of our lives (every thought, every motive, every intention)...what did we do with what we knew? All religions indeed lead to God—as Judge! (It won't be Buddha, Mohammed, or any of the Pagan gods that will be sitting as judge.) The Father has given all authority to Jesus Christ.[8]

CHRISTOPHER W. MORGAN

The following description of Hell [referring to the section in his book after this quote] recurs throughout nearly all New Testament writers. Every author pictures Hell as just punishment or judgment....So the three predominant pictures of Hell that emerge from this study are Hell as punishment, destruction, and banishment.[9]

ROBERT A. PETERSON

At death the souls of the saved go immediately into the joyous presence of Christ in heaven, while the souls of the lost go immediately into an intermediate hell...at the Last Judgment...eternal punishment for the wicked in the lake of fire.[10]

O. C. QUICK, REGIUS PROFESSOR OF THEOLOGY AT OXFORD

The strain of antiuniversalist teaching in the New Testament can hardly be regarded by an impartial mind as other than conclusive.[11]

SOLOMON STODDARD (GRANDFATHER OF JONATHAN EDWARDS)

The fear of Hell restrains men from sin. Hell is compared to Sodom, when it was all on fire (Rev. 21:8). Whatever the miseries of Hell are, they will be eternal. The duration of their misery cannot be measured....This makes every part of their misery infinite....Men may well say, "Who can dwell with everlasting burnings."[12]

WESTMINSTER CONFESSION OF FAITH

The souls of the righteous, being then made perfect in holiness, are received into the highest heavens....The souls of the wicked are cast into Hell, where they remain in torments and utter darkness, reserved to the judgment of the great day. Besides these two places for souls separated from their bodies, the scripture acknowledgeth none.[13]

WESTMINSTER LARGER CATECHISM

The punishments of sin in the world to come, are everlasting separation from the comfortable presence of God, and most grievous torments in soul and body, without intermission, in hell fire forever.[14]

APPENDIX B NOTES

1. "Eternal Punishment," position paper of the General Counsel of the Assemblies of God (USA), adopted by the Assemblies of God General Presbytery, August 17, 1976.

2. "The Final State of Man," Coral Ridge Presbyterian Church Theological Statement.

3. Donnelly, *Heaven and Hell*, 55.

4. Ibid., 53.

5. Jonathan Edwards, *The Complete Works of Jonathan Edwards*, chapter 2, "Of Endless Punishment: Concerning the Endless Punishment of Those Who Will Die Impenitent," accessed January 16, 2017, http://www.ccel.org/ccel/edwards/works2.xi.ii.html.

6. *Christian Theology*, 2nd ed., 1243.

7. John MacArthur, *The MacArthur Bible Commentary* (Nashville: Nelson Books, 2005), 111, s.v. Matthew 25:31–45.

8. Chuck Missler, "A Timely Study, the Epistles of John," tape series on John 5:27, from Koinonia House Online, accessed January 16, 2017, http://khouse.org/articles/2001/384/.

9. Morgan, *Hell Under Fire*, 142.

10. Peterson, *Hell on Trial*, 168.

11. J. I. Packer, *Hell Under Fire*, 183.

12. Solomon Stoddard, *The Fear of Hell Restrains Men From Sin*, ed. Don Kistler (Morgan, PA: Soli Deo Gloria Publications, 2003), 16–17.

13. Westminster Confession of Faith, chapter 23, "Of the State of Man After Death and the Resurrection of the Dead," accessed January 16, 2017, http://www.reformed .org/documents/.

14. Westminster Larger Catechism, Question 29, accessed January 16, 2017, http://www.reformed.org/documents/ larger1.html.

BIBLIOGRAPHY

BOOKS

American Heritage Dictionary of the English Language, The, New College Edition, edited by William Morris. Boston, MA: Houghton Mifflin Co., 1981.

Amplified Bible, The. Grand Rapids: Zondervan, 1954.

Ankerberg, John and John Weldon. *Knowing the Truth About Reality and the Bible*. Eugene, OR: Harvest House, 1997.

Barton, David. *Original Intent*. Aledo, TX: WallBuilder Press, 2000.

Baxter, Mary K. *A Divine Revelation of Hell*. New Kensington, PA: Whitaker House, 1993.

Comfort, Philip Wesley, ed. *The Origin of the Bible*. Wheaton, IL: Tyndale, 1992.

Comfort, Ray. *Hell's Best Kept Secret*. New Kensington, PA: Whitaker Press, 1989.

DeMoss, Arthur S. *The Rebirth of America*. West Palm Beach, FL: Arthur DeMoss Foundation, 1986.

Donnelly, Edward. *Biblical Teaching on the Doctrines of Heaven and Hell*. Edinburgh: The Banner of Truth Trust, 2001.

Eby, Richard E., DO. *Caught Up Into Paradise*. Grand Rapids: Fleming H. Revell, 1978.

Graham, Billy. *Angels: God's Secret Agents*. Nashville: W Publishing Group, 2000.

Graham, Franklin. *The Name*. Nashville: Thomas Nelson, 2002.

Jeffrey, Grant R. *Journey Into Eternity*. Minneapolis: Waterbrook Press, 2000.

———. *Remarkable Evidence of God's Design*. Toronto: Frontier Research Publications, 2003.

———. *The Signature of God*. Toronto: Frontier Research Publications, Inc., 1996.

Lutzer, Erwin W. *One Minute After You Die*. Chicago: Moody Press, 1997.

MacArthur, John. *The John MacArthur Study Bible*. Nashville: Thomas Nelson Bibles, 1997.

McDowell, Josh. *Evidence That Demands a Verdict*. Vol. 1. Nashville: Thomas Nelson, 1972.

———. *More Than a Carpenter*. Wheaton, IL: Tyndale House, 1977.

McDowell, Josh and Don Stewart. *Reasons Skeptics Should*

Consider Christianity. San Bernardino, CA: Here's Life Publishers, 1981.

Mears, Henrietta C. *What the Bible Is All About*. San Bernardino, CA: Regal Books, 1983.

Missler, Chuck and Nancy Missler. *Tomorrow May Be Too Late*. Coeur d'Alene, ID: The King's Highway Ministries, 2004.

Morris, Henry. *Defending the Faith*. Green Forest, AR: Master Books, 1999.

Morgan, Christopher W. and Robert A. Peterson, eds. *Hell Under Fire*. Grand Rapids: Zondervan, 2004.

Nelson's New Illustrated Bible Dictionary. Nashville: Thomas Nelson Publishers, 1995.

Peterson, Robert A. *Hell on Trial*. Phillipsburg, NJ: Presbyterian and Reformed Publishing Co., 1995.

Ryken, Leland, James C. Wilhoit, and Tremper Longman III, eds. *Dictionary of Biblical Imagery*. Downer's Grove, IL: InterVarsity Press, 1998.

Smith, Chuck. *What the World Is Coming To*. Costa Mesa, CA: The Word for Today, 1977.

Spurgeon, C. H. *The Soulwinner*. New Kensington, PA: Whitaker House, 1995.

Stanley, Charles. *Charles Stanley's Handbook for Christian Living*. Nashville: Thomas Nelson, 1996.

Stoddard, Solomon. *The Fear of Hell Restrains Men From Sin.* Morgan, PA: Soli Deo Gloria Publications, 2003.

Strobel, Lee. *The Case for Faith.* Grand Rapids: Zondervan, 2000.

Sumrall, Lester. *Run With the Vision.* Springdale, PA: Whitaker House, 1995.

———. *Alien Entities.* Springdale, PA: Whitaker House, 1995.

Strong, James. *Strong's Exhaustive Concordance.* Nashville: Abingdon, 1980.

Thompson Chain Reference Bible, The. 4th ed. Indianapolis: B. B. Kirkbride Bible Company, 1964.

Tozer, A. W. *The Knowledge of the Holy.* New York: Walker and Company, 1961.

USS Indianapolis (CA-35) Survivors. Only 317 Survived! Indianapolis: Printing Partners, 2002.

Vincent, Thomas. *Fire and Brimstone.* Morgan, PA: Soli Deo Gloria Publications, 1999.

Vine, W. E. *Vine's Expository Dictionary of Old and New Testament Words.* Grand Rapids: Fleming H. Revell & Co., 1981.

Wesley, John. *Men of Faith.* Minneapolis: Bethany House Publishers, 1943.

AUDIOVISUAL MATERIALS

Ankerberg, John. "Hell: Real or Imagined." Stealing the Mind of America Conference. 1996. ComPass International, 460 Canfield, Ste. 1000, Coeur d'Alene, ID 83814.

"Death and Beyond." Videocassette (VHS). 1993. TBN, PO Box A, Santa Ana, CA 92711. Lakewood Television Production.

Missler, Chuck. "Return of the Nephilim." Videocassette (VHS). 1998. Koinonia House, P. O. Box D, Coeur d'Alene, ID 83816-0347.

Rawlings, Dr. Maurice. "To Hell and Back." 1999. TBN, P. O. Box A, Santa Ana, CA 92711.

For further information, you may contact the author at:

Soul Choice Ministries
P. O. Box 26588
Santa Ana, CA 92799

Website: www.soulchoiceministries.org
www.facebook.com/billwiesetv
www.youtube.com/billwiesetv

If you would like to obtain Bill's testimony on CD or DVD, please visit the Soul Choice website.

CONNECT WITH US!

CHARISMA
HOUSE

(Spiritual Growth)

Facebook.com/CharismaHouse

@CharismaHouse

Instagram.com/CharismaHouse

SILOAM

(Health)

Pinterest.com/CharismaHouse

MODERN
ENGLISH
VERSION

(Bible)
www.mevbible.com